Offray

The Splendor of Ribbon

Offray

The Splendor of Ribbon

More Than 50 Glorious Ribbon Craft Projects

ELLIE SCHNEIDER

Photography by Bill Milne

FRIEDMAN/FAIRFAX
PUBLISHERS

A FRIEDMAN/FAIRFAX BOOK

Library of Congress Cataloging-in-Publication Data

Schneider, Ellie.
    Offray's the splendor of ribbon: more than 50 glorious ribbon craft projects/Ellie Schneider.
    p.   cm.
Includes bibliographical references and index.
    ISBN 1-56799-397-4
    1. Ribbon work.   2. Ribbon flowers.   I. Title.
TT850.5.S36   1997
746'.0476- -dc20   96-34089

Editor: Francine Hornberger
Art Director: Lynne Yeamans
Designer: Stephanie Bart-Horvath
Photography Director: Christopher C. Bain
Illustrations by Alan Andersen
Background Ribbon Illustrations by Susan Kemnitz
Ribbon Silhouettes by Christopher C. Bain
Photo Styling by Karin Strom
Principal Photography by Bill Milne

Color separations by Fine Arts Repro House Co., Ltd.
Printed in Singapore by KHL Printing Co Pte Ltd

Every effort has been made to present the information in this book in a clear, complete, and accurate manner.
It is important that all instructions be clearly understood before beginning a project. Please follow instructions carefully. Due to the variability of materials and skills, end results may vary. The publisher and the author
also suggest refraining from using glass, beads, or buttons on crafts intended for small children.

For bulk purchases and special sales, please contact:
Friedman/Fairfax Publishers
Attention: Sales Department
15 West 26th Street
New York, New York 10010
212/685-6610   FAX 212/685-1307

Visit our website:
http://www.metrobooks.com

Acknowledgments

It was sheer joy to work with the many talented designers who expressed their love for ribbons in the exquisite projects featured in this book. I'd like to thank the following:

Sandy Belt—Flower and Felt Pillows

Darlain J. Bohm—Tea Bag Potpourri, Stamped Party Bags and Wrappings

Shirley Botsford—Pouf Purse, Ribbon Pieced Stocking

Doris Coniglio—Victorian Apothecary Bottles, Magnolia Centerpiece, Rose Napkin Rings, Spring Swag, Party Basket

Miriam Gourley—Rainbow Notecard and Envelope, Humpty Dumpty Pillow and Wall Hanging

Nancy Keller—Woven Evening Bag

Elaine Schmidt—Bridal Topiary and Chair Swag; Ring Bearer's Pillow; Guest Book and Key to My Heart Sachet Pillow; Box and Ball Christmas Ornaments; Poinsettia, Holly and Berries; and Ribbon Rose Gift Boxes

Ginger Hansen Shafer—Wedding Box Collection and Picture Frame, Tabletop Mini-Topiaries, Woven Stocking with Button Cuff

Marlyn Siegel—Wedding Nosegay

Marinda Stewart—Ribbon-Embroidered Bed Linens, Violets in Demitasse Cup, Potted Ribbon Flowers, Rose Garland on a Chain, Sweet Pea Lamp and Shade, Bride and Bridesmaid Headpieces, Summer Hat with White Roses, Burgundy Hat with Flowers, White Beret with Ribbon Embroidery, Ribbon Flower Lapel Pins

Linda Wyszynski—Rose Splendor Slippers

Patricia Zarak—Harvest Basket, Christmas Wreath

Sheila Zent—Decorative Pillows, Tea Time Table Set

Thank you to Claude V. Offray, Jr., and to the employees at Offray for creating a product that is so inspirational to "play" with and of which we are very proud.

I'd also like to thank those who so graciously allowed us to photograph this book in their homes: Marlyn Siegel, Betsy Schweppe, and Shirley Botsford. Thanks also to the Bird and Bottle Inn in Garrison, New York; The Garden Shop in Glen Ridge, New Jersey; and to Karin Strom for her photo styling expertise in enhancing the beauty of our projects. A special thank you to Rosie's Creations, New York, New York, for the "tastefully" elegant bridal shower cookies. A very big thank you to Nancy Keller for her tireless efforts in coordinating the instructions for the projects—and of course to the patient and talented staff at the Michael Friedman Publishing Group for creating the opportunity for this beautiful book.

Contents

INTRODUCTION

8

CHAPTER ONE

GENERAL TECHNIQUES

8

12

CHAPTER TWO

AT HOME WITH RIBBONS

8

30

CHAPTER THREE

BRIDAL SPLENDOR

8

64

CHAPTER FOUR

SPECIAL OCCASIONS WITH RIBBONS

8

88

CHAPTER FIVE

RIBBON FASHIONS

8

110

SOURCES

8

126

INDEX

8

127

Introduction

⊚

Ribbon History

Exquisite ribbons, once affordable only to the French nobility of the seventeenth century, are now experiencing renewed interest and adoration. Not only are they beautiful to behold, wonderful to use as embellishments, and sensuous to the touch, ribbons are also used to express emotions and feelings of pride, to reward accomplishments and excellence, and to provide opportunities for hours of creative expression. Throughout our lives, ribbons are associated with special moments—birthday packages dressed with ribbons hint of the treasures to be found inside, and bridal flowers and accessories with flowing ribbon streamers add to the promise of a happy future. What would the holiday season be without red satin and velvet ribbons accenting the greenery of wreaths and garlands?

Songwriters and poets have often chosen images of ribbons to tell their stories. The symbolic yellow ribbon, so popular during the Persian Gulf War, was first associated with a Civil War ballad, "She Wore a Yellow Ribbon." With the many colors, patterns, textures, and sizes of ribbons available today, it is no wonder that they are often used with abandon, decorating our homes,

Ribbon books were used by Claudius Marie Offray, the founder of C.M. Offray and Son, Inc., to sell his beautiful ribbons in the late 1800s. This book is one of many in the Offray archives.

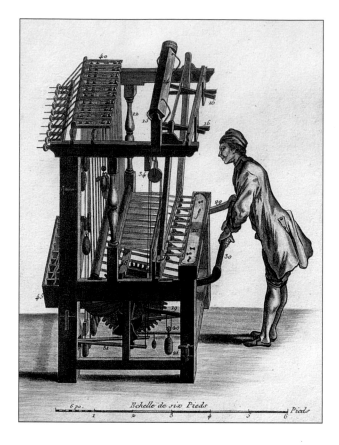

production of ribbons. The popularity of ribbons was such that the number of looms in Basle, Switzerland, a leading ribbon-producing region, went from 1,225 in 1775 to 7,631 in 1870. The introduction of the jacquard loom around 1815, which made possible lovely floral and pictorial ribbons, further expanded the use and desire for ribbons.

At the height of their popularity as a fashion embellishment during the seventeenth and eighteenth centuries, ribbons were favored by men as well as women. Shoes and hats were lavishly trimmed with ribbon rosettes and cockades. Garments were elaborately embroidered and decorated with ribbons of silk and gold. In fact, one male garment on view in London's Victoria and Albert Museum is trimmed with 250 yards (230m) of ribbons.

clothing, craft and hobby projects, and gifts and packages, as we nurture our sense of aesthetics and elegance.

Although the first ribbon factory in the United States was founded in 1815, ribbons had already been made in Europe for some time. Colonial Americans had rejected the use of ribbons due to anti-English political feelings. In France and then England, ribbons represented nobility. In fact, at one point, the English Parliament restricted the wearing of ribbons to nobility. At first, ribbons were made in the homes of peasant farmers on looms that they rented from manufacturers. The invention of an advanced loom, capable of weaving numerous ribbons at a time, heralded a breakthrough in the

TOP: *An operator weaves ribbons on an early loom.*
RIGHT: *A ribbon merchant displays his wares.*

Ladies' magazines of the late 1870s featured ribbons as important embellishments for day and evening wear, as well as on millinery.

As a ribbon lover from the first time I saw snips of ribbons, trimmings, and fabrics in my grandmother's sewing basket, I adore the many ways in which Offray's beautiful and versatile ribbons have been used to create the wide range of items featured in this book. I hope that these ideas and techniques will inspire and excite ribbon lovers everywhere to create treasures and heirlooms of their own.

Offray History

C.M. Offray and Son, Inc., has created, manufactured, and merchandised "The World's Most Beautiful Ribbons" since 1876. Claudius Marie Offray came to America from what was then the ribbon center of France, Saint-Etienne near Lyons, as a manufacturer's representative of French textiles and fancy ribbons. Offray was soon producing ribbons in its first mill in Paterson, New Jersey, the major textile region in this country. Claude V. Offray, Jr., grandson of the founder and president, currently oversees the operation of this business, which now has factories, warehouses, showrooms, and offices throughout the world. Many of the exquisite ribbons in the line today are taken from the original ribbon books that the founder used in his ribbon sales. Offray maintains the high standards established by the young Frenchman 120 years ago—beauty and excellence in a product that carries the Offray name on every spool.

Many of the techniques for ribbon manipulation that we use today in our creations are taken from these earlier examples and re-created with present-day ribbons. Ribbon roses, for instance, were very popular with our Victorian ancestors as well as their ancestors. The popular ladies' magazines of the early 1900s featured this classic Victorian flower on hair ornaments, belts and bags, lingerie items, and decorative pillows for the home. Ribbon embroidery also has its roots in the elaborate embellishments of the French and English ball gowns and accessories and was later seen in examples of fine handwork on Victorian crazy quilts.

Throughout this book, you will see the luxurious, yet readily available wire-edge ribbons made not only into roses, but also into a "garden of ribbon flowers" that will last from spring to spring. We have also updated the fine art of ribbon embroidery with our use of a washable polyester ribbon, suited to today's busy lifestyle while retaining the beauty of its original art form.

CHAPTER ONE

General Techniques

"There is nothing which adds more colorful charm to a woman's
possessions—her clothes, her children's clothes,
her home—than does ribbon."
—The Art and Craft of Ribbonwork

Before you begin your ribbon creations, be sure to take a moment to become familiar with this section of the book. For many projects, you will be given ribbon lengths and then referred back to this section for specific instructions. For example, to make pansies for the Black Pansy Pillow in chapter two, you will be referred to page 33. In addition, this section lists general supplies that you may want to have on hand. We'd also like to give you a quick lesson on the differences between the many types of ribbons available. For those of you already aware of the variety of ribbons, consider this chapter a refresher course.

There are two major classifications of ribbons on the market: woven edge and cut edge. Woven-edge ribbons are woven on a loom and have finished selvages, or edges, making them suitable for stitch-down application for apparel or crafts. These ribbons are usually washable or dry-cleanable. I recommend that you prewash both the fabric and the ribbon you will be using for any project. You will find that many of the projects featured in this book use woven-edge ribbons. These include wire-edge woven ribbons, which have a thin copper wire woven into the edges, sheer ribbons, metallic ribbons, and printed and patterned ribbons. If you are not sure whether a ribbon is woven, just look for a finished selvage.

The other type of ribbon, cut-edge or craft ribbon, is made from fabric that has been slit into ribbon widths and treated with a stiffening agent to give it body. This ribbon is suitable for craft and floral projects and can be glued or wired as desired. Cut-edge ribbon is not recommended for projects that are to be washed. Within this category, you will also find a type of wire ribbon. This is called a merrowed-edge wire ribbon because the wire has been attached with a merrowing stitch that finishes the slit or cut edge of the ribbon. Cotton print ribbons, textured ribbons, tapestry-type ribbons, and other novelties are among those you will find in the cut-edge ribbon classification.

General Supplies and Equipment

Here are some general supplies and equipment you will want to have on hand before beginning your adventures in ribbon crafting:

- scissors
- thread
- needle
- glue gun
- glue sticks
- green floral tape
- needle nose pliers with built-in wire cutters

- 18-, 24-, and 30-gauge green floral stem wire
- glue (E6000, Goop, or equivalent)
- ruler
- tape measure
- Oasis floral foam or Styrofoam blocks

- sheet moss
- floral craft pins (U-shaped pins to secure moss)

- size 5 or 6 (3¾ mm or 4mm) knitting needle or size 16 pennynail or equivalent.

Use Royal Coat decoupage finish or Mod Podge by Plaid for gluing ribbon to box surfaces and for covering mat with fabric. Hot glue is used to attach heavier ribbons and satin roses.

General Embroidery Techniques and Stitches

Before getting started, consider these general embroidery tips and review the stitches illustrated below:

- Make your first stitch a backstitch to secure the ribbon. End off ribbon by weaving it behind the stitches or leaving a tail to be caught by the next stitch.

- For best results, keep ribbon lengths short, approximately 12 inches (30.5cm).
- It is very important to keep ribbon flat while stitching.
- Use a tapestry needle or embroidery needle with an eye large enough to accommodate the width of ribbon.

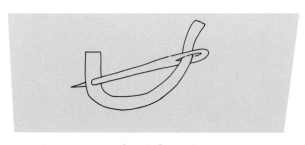

Lock Stitch

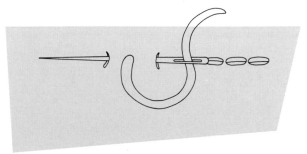

Backstitch

Running Stitch

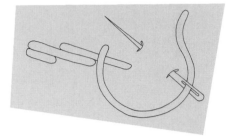

Stem Stitch

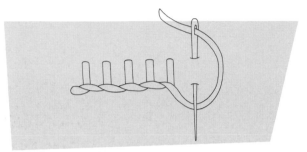

Blanket Stitch

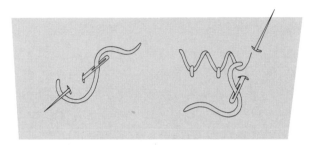

Fly Stitch

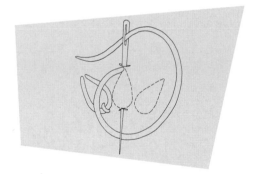

Lazy Daisy Stitch

Chain Stitch

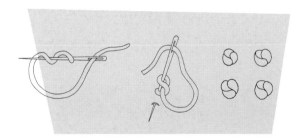

French Knot

Japanese Flower Stitch

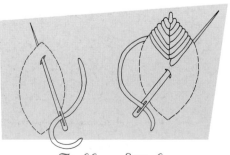

Fishbone Stitch

General Bow Techniques

T W O - L O O P   B O W

(Build on two-loop bow to make four-, six-, and eight-loop bows.)

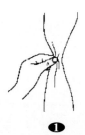

❶   **❷**   **❸**

Cut a length of ribbon as directed. Wrap the ribbon back and forth, forming two loops with tails. Glue small strip of ribbon around ribbon loops to hold in place. Ease the ribbon tail to the back of the bow.

For four- and six-loop bows, simply increase the number of loops before securing the center strip.

NOTE: When using ombre ribbon, results will differ depending on which side you work. Experiment with this for interesting color variations.

F L O R I S T   B O W

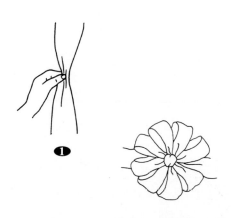

❶   **❷**   **❸**

❹   **❺**

Begin by leaving a tail length of at least 8 inches (20.5cm), and pinch at center between thumb and index finger. Bring ribbon up and back down, forming a loop. Gather firmly between thumb and index finger. Twist the ribbon, and then bring ribbon down and back up to form another loop, and again pinch and twist it into place between thumb and index finger. Repeat the process of forming loops until you have made the desired number of loops. Secure loops by wrapping center with wire. Fasten wire and twist the bow a few turns in the same direction to finish. Adjust bow loops. Notch or trim ends. A center loop may be added if desired.

General Flower Techniques

HOW TO ATTACH A FLOWER TO A STEM

Cut stem wire to desired length. With needle nose pliers, bend a small loop at one end of wire. The loop will be concealed with the stamens or in the center of the flower and will help prevent flower head from easily being removed. Attach stem wire to stamens (if used) with floral tape. If not using stamens, conceal loop in the center of a petal. Wrap petal to stem wire below loop. Attach with fine floral wire, then cover with green floral tape.

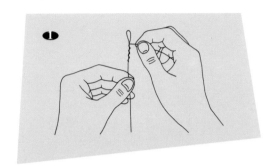

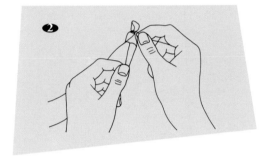

FOLDED LEAF

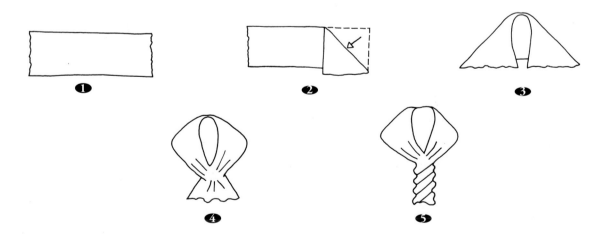

Cut ribbon to desired length. Mark center of ribbon and fold each end diagonally to center mark. At lower edge, fold each side of ribbon toward center. Gently pleat fullness at lower edge to center. Twist tightly to hold. Secure twist with floral tape. To attach leaf, use floral tape and wrap on twisted end of ribbon.

PULLED LEAF OR PETAL

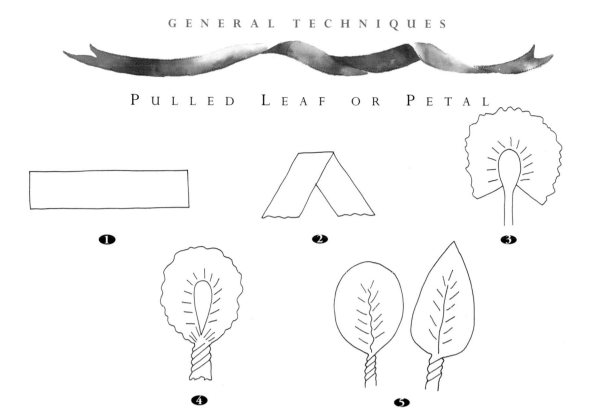

Cut wire-edge ribbon to desired length for each leaf or petal. Fold in half. Gather one edge of ribbon by pulling both ends of the wire from the cut ends at the same time; this prevents you from accidentally pulling wire out of ribbon. Push all gathers to the center of the ribbon. Overlap the ends of the ribbon and, with wire exposed, tightly wrap the ends together to hold. If desired, apply a small line of glue down the center seam to hold the leaf or petal closed. The ends of the leaf or petal can be left rounded or pinched to a point as desired.

ROLLED PETAL

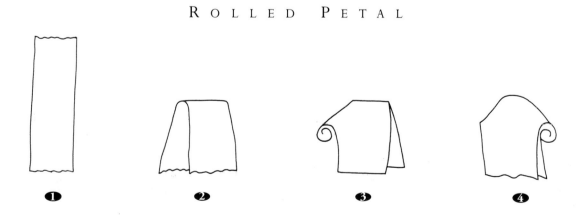

Cut ribbon to desired length. Fold in half. With a knitting needle or equivalent, gently roll each edge at the fold. Roll at a 45-degree angle. When attaching petal, gently pleat lower edge so petal will "cup." Petals are placed with rolled edges facing away from center of flower.

R O L L E D   P E T A L   R O S E

Make petals in same manner as rolled petals (see page 19). Assemble by attaching a stamen to a 4-inch (10cm) wire with a loop. Add drop of glue to hold stamen. Cover with floral tape. When using petals of different widths, begin with smaller widths and use larger widths for second half of rose. For round one, evenly space three petals around stamen. Overlap petals. Secure with floral wire. For rosebuds, stop after one round. For round two, add five petals evenly spaced around base. On round three, add four petals to top, bottom, and each side. Finally, for round four, finish with remaining four petals. Offset these petals in between previous ones. Secure all rounds with floral wire. Cover all raw edges with floral tape.

S T I T C H E D   O R   " B O A T "   L E A F   P E T A L

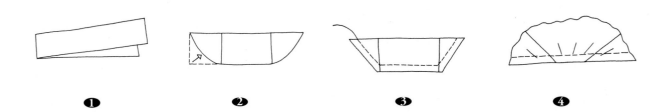

❶   ❷   ❸   ❹

Cut ribbon to desired length. Fold in half. Fold corners to center at 45-degree angle (result will give a boatlike shape). With needle and thread, knot one end and begin stitching at top edge of fold through all thicknesses down angled edge, across lower edge, and up the other side. Gently pull stitches to gather ribbon into a some-what straight line. Knot to secure. Trim excess ribbon from folds. Open ribbon to make leaf or petal.

NOTE: Experiment with ombre ribbon for interesting color variations.

STITCHED AND GATHERED PETALS

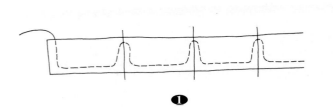

❶   ❷   ❸

Cut ribbon to length as directed. Measure and mark on ribbon the correct length of each petal. With needle and matching thread, stitch ribbon as illustrated. Every two to three petals, gently but firmly gather the stitches together to make petals. Repeat along entire length of ribbon. Pull all gathers together firmly. Knot thread to secure. Arrange petals into a circle and join. If desired, sew across space at center to close. Thread stamen wire through center of flower and secure in place. If necessary, use floral tape to attach flower to stem wire.

TWISTED STEM

Measure and cut ribbon as directed. Twist ribbon tightly between fingers. Secure each end with glue or handstitches.

FANCY ROSE

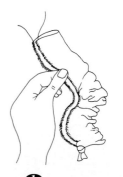

❶   ❷   ❸

Measure and cut ribbon as directed. Knot one end; pull knot firmly toward end to secure. Hold ribbon at opposite end and poke out wires from both sides of ribbon. Fold ribbon in half lengthwise and push ribbon down length of wire toward the knot, forming a tight gathered ruffle. Keep both layers together as one. Form rose by rolling gathered edge around knot. Continue wrapping ribbon around to achieve desired look. Secure ends.

GATHERED ROSE

❶   ❷   ❸

Measure and cut ribbon as directed. Knot one end; pull knot firmly toward end to secure. From opposite side, gently pull one wire, slowly gathering ribbon along that edge. Continue gathering until entire side is completely ruffled and curling naturally. Wrap gathered ribbon around knotted end, forming bud. Continue wrapping lightly so ribbon flares out and acquires an open rose effect. Tie wires together and trim. Adjust shape by fluffing or crumpling.

DAFFODIL CENTER

 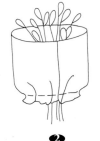

❶   ❷

Cut ribbon lengths as directed. Join raw ends of one length to form a ring, and stitch in a ⅛-inch (3mm) seam. Fold so seam is in center. With running stitch, gather tube tightly along one edge of ribbon. Pull stitches together tightly and knot securely. Insert stamen into center of tube and glue.

DAHLIA

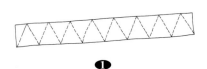 

❶   ❷

Sew with matching thread in a zigzag fashion. Pull stitches together tightly. Tack points and centers in place. Stitch four or five French knots in center with gold Silk-Ease embroidery ribbon. For buds, use 3-inch (7.5cm) lengths of ribbon and reduce the number of zigzags.

HOLLY LEAVES AND BERRIES

leaves ❶

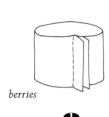

berries ❶

❷

❸

To make holly leaves, cut three 4-inch (10cm) lengths of green ribbon. Cut one end of each length into a point. Pinch remaining ends of lengths together and wire to form leaf shapes. To make berries, cut three 4-inch (10cm) lengths of red ribbon. Overlap cut ends of each length to form a ring and glue. Sew gathering stitches along one edge of ribbon and pull tightly. Knot thread and turn berry inside out to hide stitches. Stuff berry with cotton or Fiberfil. Gather remaining edge of ribbon. Pull tightly and knot thread.

HYACINTH

❶

❷

❸

Make one small loop at one end of 9-inch (23cm) length of stem wire. Cut lengths as directed and fold in half to form petals. Assemble hyacinth by placing first petal over the top of stem wire. Secure with floral tape. Place three petals evenly spaced approximately ½ to ⅝ inch (1.5cm) below top loop and attach with floral tape. Repeat for rows 3, 4, 5, and 6, increasing by one petal each row. For rows 7 and 8, use seven petals each. For rows 9, 10, 11, and 12, use eight petals each. Repeat as needed for each hyacinth spike.

IRIS

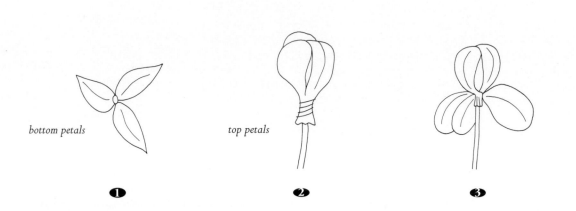

bottom petals   *top petals*

❶   ❷   ❸

Cut ribbon as directed. Make three boat leaves from longer lengths and make three pulled leaves from shorter lengths. To make "beard," glue a ¾-inch (2cm) length of yellow chenille over center seam of each pulled leaf. Assemble iris by clustering three boat leaf petals with right sides together. Glue three petals together to hold. Fold petals to right side. Gather base of petals around a 4-inch (10cm) stem wire. Secure. Add three pulled petals, beard side up, to flower center. Evenly space petals. Secure. Cover all raw edges with floral tape.

MORNING GLORY

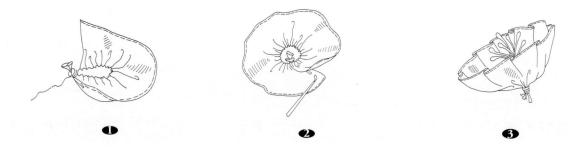

❶   ❷   ❸

Measure and cut ribbon as directed. Make tight knot in one end. Gather ribbon by pulling wire from other end. Wrap ends of gathering wire together to secure. Pleat outer edge to form a cup shape. Insert a stamen through the center of flower. Wrap each center around stamen and glue closed.

PANSY

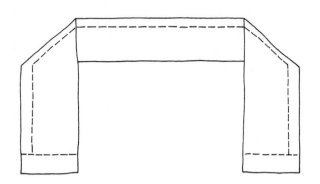

Cut ribbon in 7½-inch (19cm) lengths. Fold and twist each end down: 2¼ inches (6cm), 3 inches (7.5cm), 2¼ inches (6cm). Sewing with regular thread on dotted lines, start at one end and sew along all outer edges. Pull tight. Sew raw edges together. Using 4mm gold Silk-Ease, make long, straight stitches in flower centers. For buds, use 1¾-inch (4.5cm) lengths of ribbon and only one fold.

POINSETTIA

To form inner petals, cut three 6-inch (15cm) lengths of ribbon. Cut ends into sharp points. Pinch the lengths at the center and wire the three lengths together. Shape petals into a circle. To form outer petals, cut four 8-inch (20.5cm) lengths of ribbon. Cut the ends of each into a sharp point. Pinch the lengths at the center and shape into a circle. Wire outer petals together. Next wire inner and outer petals together. Glue beads in center.

SWEET PEA

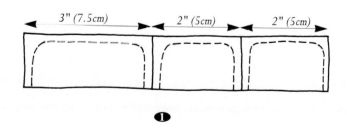

3" (7.5cm)   2" (5cm)   2" (5cm)

❶

❷

Measure and cut ribbon as instructed. Sew petals in the same manner as stitched and gathered petals. To assemble sweet peas, tack the larger petal to one side of the smaller petal. Next bar-tack the two small petals together. The smaller petals should face each other with the larger petal cupped at the back. For variety, use both sides of colored edges on ombre ribbons.

General Stamping Techniques

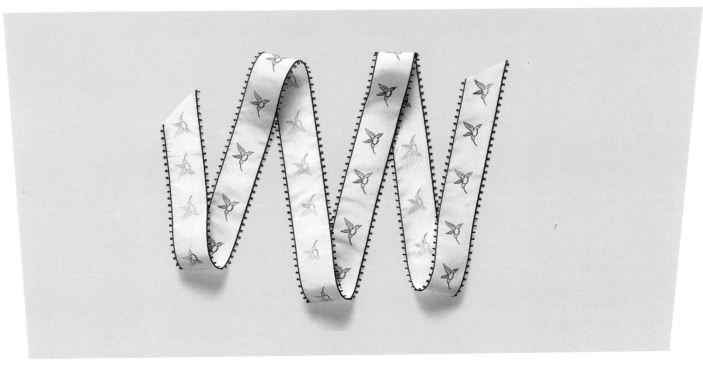

There are two basic types of ink available for stamping: permanent and heat-set permanent. The heat-set ink usually comes in a bottle for application with a pad. The permanent comes with a built-in sponge top or ball applicator fed by squeezing.

To prevent a fuzzy final appearance, keep the ink from running into the grooves of the stamp. This can easily be done on the sponge top: saturate the sponge top then set the bottle upright. Gently tap your stamp against the sponge top. Try to keep your pad from becoming too full, and do not press stamp too hard on the pad. To ensure even distribution of ink across entire stamp, you may want to use a small sponge brush. Practice applying pressure on stamp to determine best method. Small compact stamps need even, central pressure. Narrow and elongated stamps need pressure distributed carefully around all edges and center to achieve an even result.

Although any width of ribbon can be stamped, wider ribbons will allow for more flexibility in choosing various size stamps.

Ribbons take very well to either ink. Most natural fibers fully absorb ink, while polyester and synthetic ribbons will hold ink best. Before stamping the ribbon, practice on another surface repeatedly until you achieve the desired result.

A word of caution: lay out ribbon on an absorbent, disposable material, such as paper towels, when stamping. Ink can soak through ribbon as well as paper and fabric, so be prepared.

General Weaving Techniques

The techniques described below for weaving and on page 29 for strip piecing provide more opportunities to be creative with ribbon. From these techniques you will be able to create your own fabric for various projects or simply embellish parts of projects. Once you have tried these methods and realize how quick and easy they are, there will be no limit to the uses you will find. For variety, change the widths and types of ribbons in each project.

BASIC WEAVE AND VARIATIONS

Cut lengths of ribbon and fusible interfacing as instructed in individual projects. Place fusible interfacing, fusible side up, on a pinnable work surface—a purchased pinning board, ironing board, or fabric-covered cardboard. Draw the required dimensions on the interfacing. Place first vertical length of ribbon (warp) on interfacing, aligning edge of ribbon with line on interfacing. Butt edges of remaining warp ribbons and pin at upper end of ribbons. Angle pins away from work to keep pins clear of iron when fusing. Weave horizontal lengths of

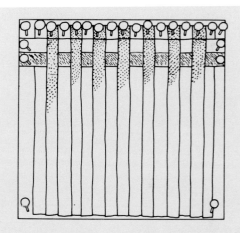

When you insert the horizontal ribbons, it will look like this.

ribbons (weft) one over, one under vertical ribbons, continuing across. When row is complete, push weft ribbon up to top seam marking, ensuring ribbon is straight and taut. Pin ends in place. Continue weaving weft ribbons until project is complete. Every row should be pulled taut and straight, butting edges with previous weft ribbon, before starting next row. Fuse ribbons to interfacing following manufacturer's instructions. Stitch along outer edges of ribbons on all four sides to secure ribbons in place. Stitching is especially important with metallic ribbons since they do not fuse well.

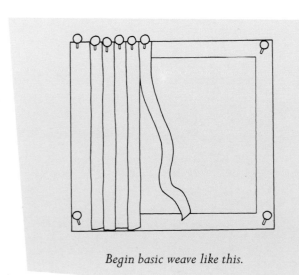

Begin basic weave like this.

THREE-DIMENSIONAL RIBBON WEAVE PROJECTS

To form a tumbling blocks pattern, use one ribbon for warp and a different one for each set of diagonal ribbons. To form hexagons, alternate three ribbons throughout entire weaving process.

Pin interfacing, fusible side up, to ironing board or padded work surface. Center the warp ribbons vertically on the interfacing. Pin each ribbon at the top and bottom edge, pushing pins through ribbon and interfacing and into the ironing board.

Using a bodkin, weave over one warp, under two warps, over one, and so on. The ribbon should lie at a 30-degree angle from the warp ribbons. Pin each diagonal row at the ends to secure. Continue to weave rows over one and under two, so that diamonds appear from upper left to lower right. (See step one.)

Using a bodkin, weave in the second set of diagonal ribbons, from lower left to upper right. (See step two.) In each row, go over two warps and all first set of diagonal ribbons. Diamonds of ribbon will form to complete the pattern. (See step three.)

Follow manufacturer's instructions to fuse ribbons to interfacing. Machine-stitch the edges of weaving to secure all ribbon ends.

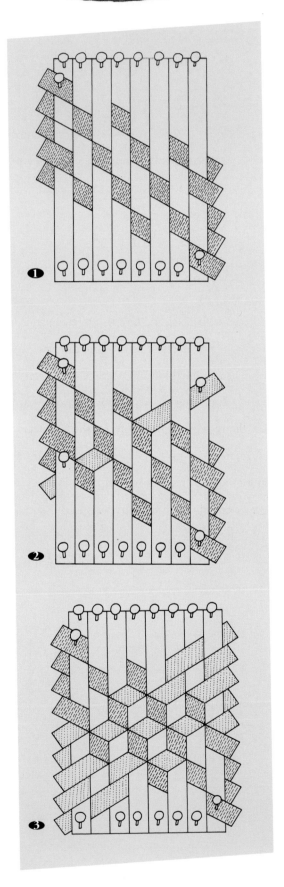

General Strip Piecing Techniques

Woven-edge ribbons are excellent for strip piecing work. They have two finished edges and are easily applied by hand, machine, or fusing, providing depth and texture. By following a few simple steps, you can make beautiful creations.

- Always work in same direction on both edges to prevent puckering.
- Ribbon is best applied to flat fabric before the garment is made up.
- Butt edges of ribbons carefully when stitching to create a smooth, even finish.

Strip piecing can be done in two methods for two different looks. The first method involves stitching the ribbon to lightweight fabric to give a firm, stable surface. For interesting treatments, try stitching sheers over colored fabrics, as seen in the Ribbon Pieced Stocking on page 92. The second method is to zigzag or featherstitch over the edges of both ribbons at the same time. This method gives a softer look as seen in the Pouf Purse on page 114. Both methods can be further embellished with decorative stitches and threads.

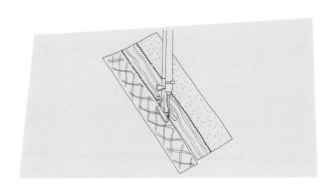

TO STRIP PIECE

Cut ribbons in lengths as directed in individual project. Set zigzag or featherstitch to a narrow width and a length long enough to catch both ribbon edges. Hold two ribbon lengths with edges butted, and zigzag or featherstitch entire length of ribbons. Continue adding ribbons to outer edges in correct order until the required size is obtained. Treat joined and sewn ribbons as fabric and continue with individual project.

TO STRIP PIECE ON FABRIC

Cut ribbons in lengths as directed in individual project. Mark a design line on fabric with disappearing marker, drawing toward center of project. Lay ribbon along the line and hold in place with a fabric glue stick or basting stitch. Straight-stitch along both edges. Butt edges of next ribbon with edge of first ribbon and anchor with glue or basting before stitching along both edges. Continue working from center to edges. Trace pattern to be cut on ribbon-trimmed fabric and stitch on traced line. Cut just outside of traced line. Continue with individual project.

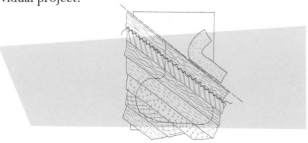

CHAPTER TWO

At Home
with Ribbons

"Let me tell you how the sun rose, a ribbon at a time…"

—Emily Dickinson

Medium Heart Pillow with Dahlias, Large Heart Pillow with Pansies, Black Pansy Pillow, Small Heart Pillow with Pansies

❁

Black Pansy Pillow

Brightly colored pansies on a field of soft felt will create a perfect accent pillow for a sofa or armchair.

RIBBON

- ¼ yard (23cm) each of 1½-inch-wide (4cm) wire-edge ombre ribbon in 3 coordinating flower colors
- 1 yard (1m) of ⅞-inch-wide (2cm) wire-edge ombre ribbon in green
- 1 package of 4mm Silk-Ease embroidery ribbon in gold

OTHER MATERIALS

- ¼ yard (23cm) of black felt
- 1 skein #5 gold pearl cotton
- Size 20 chenille needle
- Fiberfil
- Teacup

INSTRUCTIONS

1. Cut two 6-by-11-inch (15 by 28cm) pieces of felt for pillow front and back. Using a teacup as a guide, round corners.

2. From wider wire-edge ribbon, make 3 pansies as instructed on page 25. Tack pansies to pillow front, bending and crushing to look like real flowers.

3. With 11-inch (28cm) lengths of green ombre ribbon, make 3 twisted stems as instructed on page 21. Shape and tack stems to pillow, hiding ends.

4. With wrong sides together and raw edges even, stitch front to back ½-inch (1.5cm) from edge, using gold pearl cotton in a long running stitch and leaving an opening for stuffing. Stuff pillow with Fiberfil and complete running stitch to close opening. Blanket-stitch (see page 16) around outside edges of pillow using pearl cotton.

❁

Large Heart Pillow with Dahlias

By simply gathering ribbons in a zigzag effect, you can create a fresh bed of dahlias to last all summer long.

RIBBON

- ⅜ yard (34.5cm) each of 1½-inch-wide (4cm) wire-edge ombre ribbon in 3 coordinating colors
- 1 yard (1m) of ⅞-inch-wide (2cm) wire-edge ombre ribbon in green
- 1 package each of 4mm Silk-Ease embroidery ribbon in white and gold (for center)

OTHER MATERIALS

- ⅜ yard (34.5cm) of white felt
- 1 skein #5 green pearl cotton
- Fiberfil

INSTRUCTIONS

1. Cut 2 pieces of felt in heart shape, approximately 13 by 11 inches (33 by 28cm).

2. Make 3 dahlias from 13-inch (33cm) lengths of 1½-inch-wide (4cm) ribbon, following instructions on page 22. Make 3 dahlia buds from each of the 3 remaining lengths.

3. Cut three 10-inch (25.5cm) lengths of green ombre ribbon. Make a twisted stem for each dahlia, following instructions on page 21.

4. Arrange flowers, buds, and stems on pillow front and tack in place. Make French knots from gold Silk-Ease ribbon in centers. Cover raw edges of stems and buds with long straight stiches and white Silk-Ease embroidery ribbon.

5. Use green pearl cotton to blanket-stitch (see page 16) front to back, wrong sides together and raw edges even, leaving an opening for stuffing. Stuff pillow with Fiberfil and then blanket-stitch around edges to complete.

Small Heart Pillow with Pansies

Pansies and buds in fresh spring colors are delightful accents to this charming decorative pillow.

RIBBON

- ¼ yard (23cm) each of ⅞-inch-wide (2cm) wire-edge ombre ribbon in 3 coordinating colors
- 1 package each of 4mm Silk-Ease embroidery ribbon in gold, burgundy (for center), and green

OTHER MATERIALS

- ¼ yard (23cm) of white felt
- 1 skein #5 green pearl cotton
- Size 20 chenille needle
- Fiberfil

INSTRUCTIONS

1. Cut 2 pieces of felt in heart shape, approximately 7 by 6 inches (18 by 15cm), for pillow front and back.

2. Make 3 pansies from the ⅞-inch-wide (2cm) ribbon. See page 25 for instructions. With the remaining lengths of ribbon, make 3 pansy buds.

3. Arrange flowers and buds on pillow front and tack in place.

4. Twist and tack green Silk-Ease in place, forming a continuous stem on pillow front. Take long straight stitches across lower edge of buds, covering raw edges.

5. To finish pillow, blanket-stitch (see page 16) front to back, wrong sides together and raw edges even, using green pearl cotton. Remember to leave an opening for stuffing. Stuff pillow then complete blanket stitch around edges.

Medium Heart Pillow with Pansies

Every day can be a spring day with a heart full of pansies pillow.

RIBBON

- ⅜ yard (34.5cm) each of 1½-inch-wide (4cm) wire-edge ombre ribbon in 3 coordinating colors
- 1 yard (1m) of ⅞-inch-wide (2cm) wire-edge green ombre ribbon
- 1 package each of 4mm Silk-Ease embroidery ribbon in gold and green

OTHER MATERIALS

- ¼ yard (23cm) of white felt
- 1 skein #5 pearl green cotton
- Size 20 chenille needle
- Fiberfil

INSTRUCTIONS

1. Cut 2 pieces of felt in heart shape, approximately 11 by 9 inches (28 by 23cm), for pillow.

2. Using 7½-inch (19cm) lengths of 1½-inch-wide (4cm) ribbons, make a pansy in each of the 3 colors. See page 25 for instructions. With the remaining 3½-inch (9cm) lengths, make 3 pansy buds.

3. Using 12-inch (30.5cm) lengths of green ombre ribbon, make 3 twisted stems, following instructions on page 21.

4. Sew buds to ends of twisted stems.

5. Place and tack pansies to front pillow. Attach twisted stems and buds to pillow, hiding raw edge of stems under pansies.

6. Using Silk-Ease, make 4 or 5 straight stitches in the center of each pansy.

7. With wrong sides of pillow together and raw edges even, use pearl cotton to blanket-stitch (see page 16) front to back, leaving an opening for stuffing. Stuff pillow with Fiberfil and blanket-stitch to complete.

Victorian Apothecary Bottles

A snip of cord, soft sheer ribbons, and lace give a touch of grace and charm to ordinary bottles, turning them into romantic treasures.

RIBBON

Bottle A

- ½ yard (45.5cm) of metallic mesh ribbon
- 2 yards (2m) of sheer ribbon
- ⅜ yard (34.5cm) of gold ribbon

Bottle B

- ½ yard (45.5cm) of metallic mesh Elan ribbon
- 1 yard (1m) of wire-edge ribbon

Bottle C

- 1½ yards (1.5m) of sheer ribbon
- ½ yard (45.5cm) of gold cord

OTHER MATERIALS

- Bottles
- Lace appliqués
- Purchased ribbon roses
- Victorian pictures (from old cards or magazines)
- Charms, pearls, flowers, fruit (optional)

INSTRUCTIONS

1. For bottle A, wrap metallic mesh ribbon around the bottle and secure with rubber band around neck. Tie ribbon over rubber band and make a four-loop bow as instructed on page 17. Glue to neck of bottle. Add bow from gold ribbon. Glue 13 ribbon roses around picture on bottle label.

2. For bottle B, pull mesh ribbon apart and wrap around bottle. Weave sides together with ribbon, securing the ends of ribbon with hot glue. Secure ends of mesh ribbons in bottleneck with cork. Make a four-loop bow and glue to neck.

3. For bottle C, glue cording around bottle to back; do not glue underneath bottle. Glue lace appliqué in front. Glue ribbon roses on top. Make a four-loop bow and glue to side of bottle. Glue 11 more ribbon roses around bow and neck.

NOTE: If you wish, further embellish with charms, pearls, flowers, or fruit.

Humpty Dumpty Pillow and Wall Hanging

Darling ribbon motifs are interpreted in this playful appliquè
pillow and wall hanging that are sure to add delight to a child's nursery.

RIBBON

- 2½ yards (2.5m) of 1½-inch-wide (4cm) Humpty Dumpty specialty ribbon
- 1½ yards (1.5m) of ⅞-inch-wide (2cm) printed ribbon
- 1½ yards (1.5m) of ⅜-inch-wide (1cm) feather-edge satin ribbon
- 4 yards (4m) of ⅞-inch-wide (2cm) plaid ribbon
- 1 package each of 4mm Silk-Ease embroidery ribbon in tan, brown, and peach

OTHER MATERIALS

- Scraps of fabric for Humpty Dumpty character and background
- ⅔ yard (61cm) of fabric for backing
- Matching thread
- Fusible web with paper back
- Fabric paint for cheeks
- 12-inch (30.5cm) pillow form
- Size 20 chenille needle

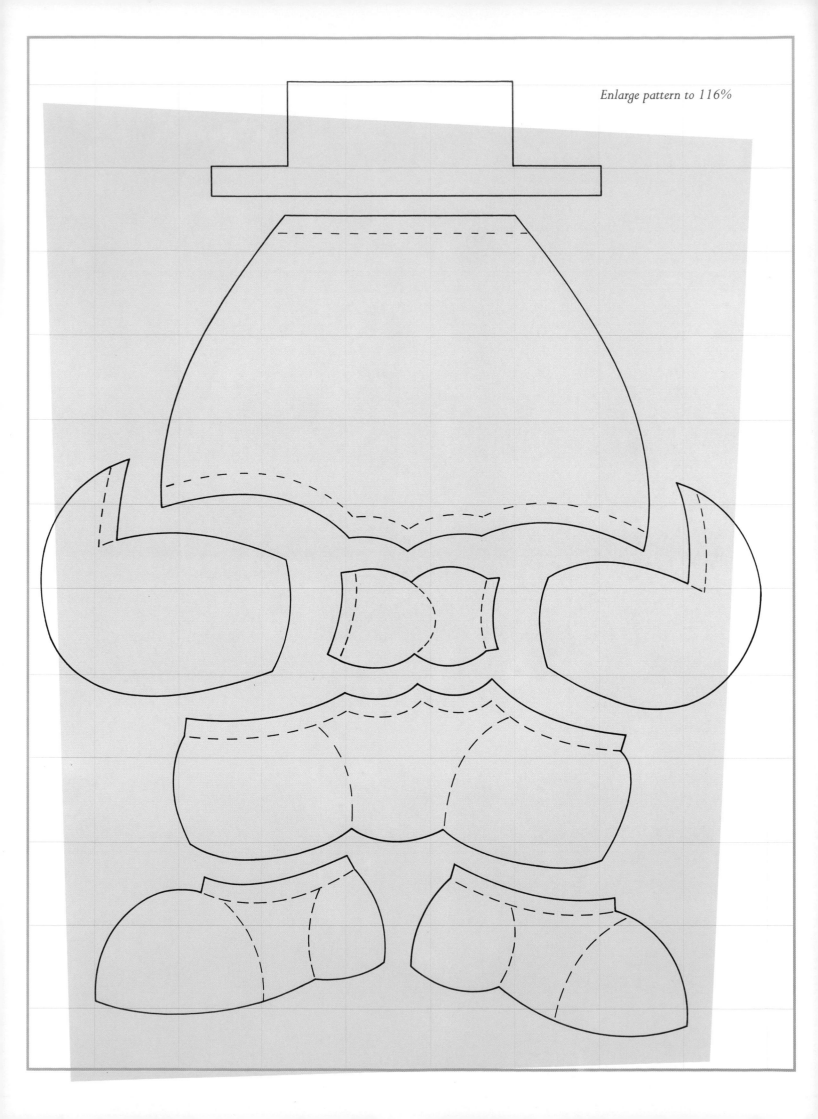

Enlarge pattern to 116%

I N S T R U C T I O N S

NOTE: Seam allowance is ½ inch (1.5cm) unless otherwise noted.

1. Trace Humpty Dumpty pattern pieces from previous page onto paper side of fusible web. Fuse the web to wrong side of fabric following manufacturer's instructions. Cut out the pieces.

2. To create the background, cut a 7¾-by-11-inch (19.5 by 28cm) rectangle from desired fabric. For the brick wall, cut a 4½-by-11-inch (11.5 by 28cm) rectangle from desired fabric. Stitch rectangles, right sides together, along 11-inch (28cm) edge. Press seam open.

3. Remove paper backing from the pattern pieces and arrange so the area of the elbow and knee are centered along the top of the wall. Fuse in place. Fuse a piece of ⅞-inch (2cm) plaid ribbon above the hat brim.

4. Use brown embroidery ribbon to outline-stitch around all sections about ⅛ inch (3mm) from edge. Use embroidery ribbon for the facial features as follows: eyes in backstitch (see page 16), brown; eyebrows in satin stitch, brown; nose in backstitch, tan; mouth in backstitch, peach; cheeks in broken outline stitch, peach.

5. Use fabric paint for cheeks, brushing on in a circular motion.

6. Make a bow tie by folding the 1½-inch-wide (4cm) ribbon so the raw ends overlap in the middle. Secure with wire or thread. Wrap a small piece of the ribbon around the center and stitch. The bow tie should be 3¾ inches (9.5cm) wide. Attach just above hands.

7. For inner border cut 4 fabric strips, two 2 by 11 inches (5 by 28cm) and two 2 by 14 inches (5 by 35.5cm).

Stitch a shorter strip to each side of square. Stitch longer strips to the top and bottom. Press seams open. Center ⅞-inch-wide (2cm) preprinted ribbon over the seam and stitch in place, mitering at corners.

8. For outer border cut 4 fabric strips, two 3 by 13 inches (7.5 by 33cm) and two 3 by 16½ inches (7.5 by 42cm). Stitch as in step 7 above. Apply feather-edge satin ribbon to outer border, just covering the seam. Center the 1½-inch-wide (4cm) printed ribbon in remaining space, inside ¼-inch (6mm) seam allowance.

9. Cut two 10-by-16½-inch (25.5 by 42cm) rectangles for back. Fold under 1-inch (2.5cm) hem on one long edge of each piece. Stitch close to fold and ⅞ inch (2cm) in from fold.

10. Place the pillow backs overlapping at finished edges. With right sides together, pin pillow back to front. Stitch, leaving an opening. Trim seams and corners. Turn right sides out and press.

11. Topstitch 2½ inches (6.5cm) from outer edges along feather-edge satin ribbon. Insert pillow form.

12. From the plaid ribbon, make 4 four-loop bows with 3-inch (7.5cm) tails. See instructions on page 17. Stitch one ribbon to each corner on top of the feather-edge satin ribbon.

NOTE: This pillow can be adapted to a wall hanging by quilting and adding ribbon loops along upper edge. Simply hang from a dowel decorated with ribbon, bows, and ivy, as shown in photograph on page 39.

CAUTION: Both pillow and wall hanging are ornamental in nature and are not meant to be placed inside a crib or where a baby might accidentally remove a bow.

Cinched Pillow with Insets

Ribbons in coordinating colors and patterns on this pillow will add a
contemporary accent to your home's decor.

RIBBON

- 1¼ yards (1m) each of 1½-inch-wide (4cm) ribbon in 5 coordinating patterns

OTHER MATERIALS

- ½ yard (45.5cm) of fabric
- Matching thread
- 16-inch (40.5cm) pillow form
- 1½ yards (1.5m) of cord

INSTRUCTIONS

NOTE: Seam allowance is ½ inch (1.5cm).

1. From fabric, cut two 10-by-17-inch (25.5 by 43cm) rectangles for pillow centers, two 8-by-17-inch (20.5 by 43cm) strips for ribbon sides, and one 4-by-17-inch (10 by 43cm) strip for center knot. From each of the ribbons, cut four 8-inch (20.5cm) strips and two 4-inch (10cm) strips.

2. Following instructions for strip piecing on page 29, stitch ribbon lengths to each 8-by-17-inch (20.5 by 43cm) fabric strip and 4-by-17-inch (10 by 43cm) center knot strip, placing ribbons horizontally across width.

3. On wrong side, draw a line through the middle of each 8-by-17-inch (20.5 by 43cm) strip. Cut along these lines to make 4 strips, each 4 by 17 inches (10 by 43cm).

4. With right sides together and matching long edges, stitch one ribbon strip to either side of the 10-by-17-inch (25.5 by 43cm) fabric panels to make two 17-inch (43cm) squares for pillow front and back.

5. With right sides together, stitch pillow front to back, leaving an opening for turning and inserting pillow. Trim seams and corners. Turn right side out and insert pillow. Slipstitch opening closed.

6. Fold remaining 4-by-17-inch (10 by 43cm) strip in half, wrong sides together, and stitch a ½-inch (1.5cm) seam on long edge. Press strip, centering seam, to form a tube 1½ by 17 inches (4 by 43cm).

7. Cinch pillow in center with cord and knot. Cover cord with ribbon tubing and slipstitch ends together.

Flanged Pillow with Ribbon Weaving, Cinched Pillow with Insets, Tufted Pillow with Corner Ties

Flanged Pillow with Ribbon Weaving

Ribbon weaving creates an eye-catching effect on this decorative pillow.

RIBBON

- 2½ yards (2.5m) each of 1½-inch-wide (4cm) ribbons in 3 patterns (ribbons A, B, C)
- 2½ yards (2.5m) each of ⅝-inch-wide (1.5cm) grosgrain ribbons in 3 colors (ribbons D, E, F)
- 4 yards (4m) of ⅞-inch-wide (2cm) grosgrain ribbon

OTHER MATERIALS

- 1 yard (1m) of moiré fabric
- Matching thread
- ⅝ yard (57cm) of batting
- ⅝ yard (57cm) of interfacing
- 14-inch (35.5cm) pillow form

INSTRUCTIONS

1. From fabric, cut one 14-inch (35.5cm) square and two 19-inch (48cm) squares. From batting, cut one 14-inch (35.5cm) and one 19-inch (48cm) square. From interfacing, cut one 19-inch (48cm) square.

2. Baste square of interfacing to wrong side of one 19-inch (48cm) square of fabric. Draw a 3½-inch (9cm) border around all 4 sides of square. This area will be woven with ribbons. (See page 27 for General Weaving Techniques.)

3. Lightly draw a diagonal line from upper right corner to lower left corner. Beginning with the first grosgrain ribbon, ribbon D, pin length directly over line, extending ½ inch (1.5cm) outside of pillow corner and ½ inch (1.5cm) inside of border marking. Repeat for opposite corner.

4. Lay lengths of ribbon A along one side of grosgrain, leaving ¼ inch (6mm) between edges and extending lengths ½ inch (1.5cm) outside and inside of border. Repeat with ribbon B, then ribbon E. Continue in this order, pinning lengths of ribbons diagonally across border, alternating pattern to cover entire front border.

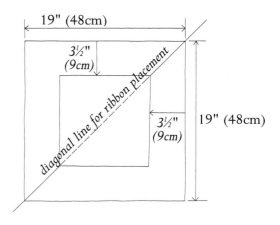

Make sure ribbon lengths are all parallel. Adjust spaces between ribbons so gaps are equal.

5. Weave second ribbon layer over and under first layer to achieve a three-dimensional weave as instructed on page 28. Continue until entire border is covered with woven ribbons. Adjust space between ribbons as needed.

6. Anchor ribbons by basting around all edges. Trim all excess ends of ribbons.

7. Baste 19-inch (48cm) square of batting to wrong side of remaining 19-inch (48cm) fabric square. Trim batting within seam allowance. With wrong sides together, baste 19-inch (48cm) fabric squares together along outside edges.

8. Press entire length of ⅞-inch (2cm) grosgrain in half lengthwise to form edge binding. Hem ⅜ inch (1cm) on one raw edge and press in place.

9. Bind all 4 edges of the 14-inch (35.5cm) square with folded ⅞-inch (2cm) grosgrain ribbon. Stitch in place, mitering at corners. Bind outside raw edges of 19-inch (48cm) square in same manner with remaining folded grosgrain.

10. With right sides up, center 14-inch (35.5cm) square on top of 19-inch (48cm) square, covering all ribbon edges. Topstitch 14-inch (35.5cm) square in place just inside of binding, leaving an opening for inserting the pillow. Insert pillow. Slipstitch opening closed.

Tufted Pillow with Corner Ties

*Contrasting cream and ivory ribbons with rich warm brown ribbons creates a
lovely accent for this bed or sofa pillow.*

NOTE: Seam allowance is ½ inch (1.5cm) unless otherwise noted.

RIBBON

- 4½ yards (4.5m) of 1½-inch-wide (4cm) jacquard (ribbon A)
- 3 yards (3m) each of 1½-inch-wide (4cm) jacquard in two patterns (ribbons B, C)
- 12 yards (11m) of ⅛-inch-wide (3mm) ribbon

OTHER MATERIALS

- ¾ yard (69cm) of 54-inch-wide (1.5m) fabric
- Matching regular and heavy-duty threads
- 16-inch (40.5cm) pillow form

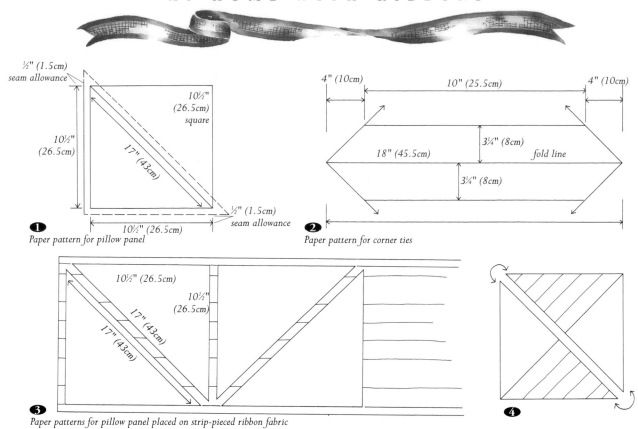

① Paper pattern for pillow panel

② Paper pattern for corner ties

③ Paper patterns for pillow panel placed on strip-pieced ribbon fabric

④

INSTRUCTIONS

1. Cut one 12-inch (30.5cm) length of fabric across the full width.

2. Cut ribbons into 54-inch (1.5m) lengths. Following instructions for strip piecing on page 29, stitch ribbons horizontally across the width of the 12-inch (30.5cm) fabric length, keeping ribbons within seam allowances. Begin applying ribbons ¾ inch (2cm) in from edge. Apply ribbons in this order: A, C, B, A, B, C, A. Apply ⅛-inch-wide (3mm) ribbon on top of butted edges of all ribbons.

3. To create paper patterns for the pillow panel, make a 10 ½-inch (26.5cm) square and fold in half to form 2 triangles. (See step 1.) Add ½-inch (1.5cm) seam allowances to 3 sides of triangles. Create paper pattern for corner ties by following measurements and illustrations in diagram. (See step 2.)

4. From ribbon fabric, cut 4 triangles, 2 corner ties, and 2 bias strips, each 5 by 10 inches (13 by 25.5cm). See above diagram for proper placement of pattern pieces. (See step 3.) Cut 4 additional triangles from plain fabric.

5. Machine-stitch ribbon triangle to plain fabric triangle on one edge. Press seam open.

6. Stitch 2 halves together to form squares for pillow front and back. Ribbons should be parallel on each panel but opposite from each other. (See step 4.)

7. With right sides together and ribbons matching, stitch pillow front to back, leaving an opening for turning. Trim seams and corners. Turn right side out. Insert pillow and slipstitch opening.

8. Fold ties in half lengthwise and stitch along raw edges leaving a 4-inch (10cm) opening for turning. Stitch each short end. Trim seams and corners. Turn right side out and slipstitch opening closed. Knot each tie. Secure to opposite corners of pillow.

9. Fold bias strips in half lengthwise and seam long ends. Turn right sides out. Tie knots in middle of both strips. Trim ends, tucking them into folds of knot. Tack securely, forming ball. Attach to center of each side of pillow. With heavy-duty thread, tuft pillow by stitching through center from front to back. Knot securely.

Violets in a Demitasse Cup

A flea market bargain can become a decorative treasure when filled with sweet ribbon violets.

RIBBON

- 1⅛ yards (2m) of ⅜-inch-wide (1cm) purple wire-edge ribbon, cut into thirteen 5-inch (13cm) lengths
- ⅝ yard (57cm) of 1½-inch-wide (4cm) green wire-edge ribbon, cut into three 7½-inch (19cm) lengths

OTHER MATERIALS

- Demitasse cup and saucer
- Floral wire
- Floral foam
- 13 single yellow stamens
- Low-temperature glue gun and glue sticks

INSTRUCTIONS

1. Glue cup to saucer. Trim floral foam to fit inside cup and glue in place.

2. Mark each length of purple wire edge ribbon at 1-inch (2.5cm) intervals for 5 petals. Following instructions for stitched and gathered petals on page 21, make 13 violets. Thread end of stamen through center of flower and attach flower to 3-inch (7.5cm) stem wire. Glue in place.

3. Following instructions on page 19, make 3 pulled leaves from 1½-inch-wide (4cm) green ribbon. Attach each leaf to 3-inch (7.5cm) stem wire with floral tape.

4. Evenly space leaves around edge of cup. Arrange violets in foam, trimming stem wire as needed.

Geraniums in a Terra Cotta Pot

You don't need a green thumb to grow these lovely ribbon geraniums.

RIBBON

- 2⅞ yards (2.5m) of ⅝-inch-wide (1.5cm) red wire-edge ribbon
- 1¼ yards (1m) of 1½-inch-wide (4cm) green ombre wire-edge ribbon, cut into five 9-inch (23cm) lengths

OTHER MATERIALS

- 4-inch (10cm) terra cotta pot
- 15 single red stamens
- Floral foam
- Sheet moss
- Low-temperature glue gun and glue sticks

INSTRUCTIONS

1. Cut red ribbon into 15 lengths, each 6¼ inches (16cm). Mark each length for five 1¼-inch (3cm) petals. Following instructions on page 21 for stitched and gathered petals, make 15 flowers. Glue single red stamen in center of each. Attach flowers to 3-inch (7.5cm) lengths of stem wire. For buds, cut remaining red ribbon into six 1¼-inch (3cm) lengths. Make 6 folded leaves as instructed on page 18, and mount to stems.

2. Center 7 or 8 blossoms and 3 buds on stem wire. Attach with floral wire. Pull individual flowers into a head of geraniums. Buds should be gently bent downward beneath head.

3. Following instructions on page 19, make 5 pulled leaves from green ombre ribbon. Use the wire on the dark edge for gathering; outer edge of leaf should be light. Leaf should be rounded. Attach 2 leaves to 1 stem. Attach 3 leaves to remaining stem.

4. Trim floral foam to fit pot. Glue in place. Cover with sheet moss. Insert geraniums into foam.

Daffodils in a Terra Cotta Pot

You can bring a touch of spring indoors with a pot of ribbon daffodils.

RIBBON

- 2⅛ yards (2m) of 1½-inch-wide (4cm) yellow ombre wire-edge ribbon

- 2 yards (2m) of ⅞-inch-wide (2cm) green ombre wire-edge ribbon, cut into six 12-inch (30.5cm) lengths

Hyacinths in a Terra Cotta Pot, Daffodils in a Terra Cotta Pot, Geraniums in a Terra Cotta Pot

OTHER MATERIALS

- 4-inch (10cm) terra cotta pot
- 3 stamens
- Floral foam
- Sheet moss
- Floral wire
- Low-temperature glue gun and glue sticks

INSTRUCTIONS

1. From yellow ombre wire-edge ribbon, cut three 4-inch (10cm) lengths. Make 3 daffodil centers as instructed on page 22.

2. Cut remaining yellow ribbon into three 21-inch (53.5cm) lengths. Mark each length into six 3½-inch (9cm) petals. Make stitched and gathered petals as instructed on page 21, ensuring that light edge of ribbon is on outer edge of petal. Pinch end of each petal into a point.

3. Glue daffodil center to middle of petals, threading stamen wire through center of petals. Attach daffodils to 8- to 10-inch (20.5 to 25.5cm) lengths of wire.

4. From green ombre ribbon, make boat leaves as instructed on page 20. Attach 2 leaves to each daffodil stem.

5. Trim floral foam to fit pot. Glue in place. Cover with sheet moss. Insert daffodils into foam, staggering heights.

Hyacinths in a Terra Cotta Pot

Three shades of purple ribbon form the loopy petals of these springtime flowers that you can enjoy year-round.

RIBBON

- 6 yards (5.5m) each of ⅜-inch-wide (1cm) wire-edge ribbon in 3 shades of purple
- 2 yards (2m) of ⅞-inch-wide (2cm) wire-edge green ombre ribbon, cut into six 12-inch (30.5cm) lengths

OTHER MATERIALS

- 4-inch (10cm) terra cotta pot
- Floral foam
- Sheet moss
- Floral wire
- Low-temperature glue gun and glue sticks

INSTRUCTIONS

1. Make a small loop at one end of 9-inch (23cm) length of stem wire.

2. Cut ⅜-inch (1cm) wire-edge ribbon into 3-inch (7.5cm) lengths, approximately 70 to 72 pieces of each color. Make 3 hyacinth spikes in each shade of purple. See page 23 for instructions.

3. Cut green ribbon into 6 lengths. Make 6 boat leaves as instructed on page 20. Attach 2 leaves to each spike stem.

4. Cut floral foam to fit pot. Glue in place. Cover with sheet moss. Trim spikes as needed. Insert into foam.

Embroidered Victorian Linens

A lovely old craft has found renewed interest when created with soft, easy-care ribbons using familiar embroidery stitches.

RIBBON

- 5 yards (4.5m) of 2¼-inch-wide (5.5cm) single-face satin ribbon
- 10 yards (9m) of ⅛-inch-wide (3mm) satin mini-dot ribbon in peach
- 3 yards (3m) of 1½-inch-wide (4cm) sheer satin striped ribbon in peach
- 2 yards (2m) each of ⅛-inch-wide (3mm) double-face satin ribbon in dusty rose and apricot
- 2 packages each of 4mm Silk-Ease embroidery ribbon in tea rose, spring moss, and moss
- 1 package each of 4mm Silk-Ease embroidery ribbon in iris, grape, and moss
- 1 package of 2mm Silk-Ease embroidery ribbon in moss

OTHER MATERIALS

- 1 queen-size flat sheet and pillowcase
- Transfer pencil
- 10 yards (9m) of 3½-inch-wide (9cm) ecru lace
- Chenille, embroidery, and crewel needles
- Matching thread

INSTRUCTIONS

1. For each pillowcase, cut 1¼ (1m) yards of 2¼-inch-wide (5.5cm) satin ribbon. Fold in half and mark center. Fold in half again to mark quarters.

2. Enlarge and center design on the following page to one side of ribbon at quarter mark. Transfer design to satin side of ribbon using transfer pencil.

3. Embroider design as indicated. Refer to page 15 for General Embroidery Techniques. Set aside.

4. Cut a 2½-yard (2.5m) length of lace and sew raw edges together to form a ring.

5. By hand or machine, gather lace to fit pillowcase. Topstitch ¼ inch (6mm) above hemline on pillowcase using a straight stitch or narrow zigzag.

6. Topstitch embroidered ribbon above lace. Overlap bottom edge of ribbon to cover stitching on lace. Overlap raw edges at seam line. Turn under any raw edges and slipstitch in place.

7. Cut two 1¼-yard (1m) lengths of peach mini-dot ribbon. Center ribbon over each side of satin stripe ribbon length. Finish as above at pillow seam.

8. Cut a 27-inch (68.5cm) length of sheer satin stripe ribbon. Tie a bow and cut ends to form a V. Sew to pillow below center rose between ribbon and lace.

9. Repeat process for sheet. Center an embroidery motif where each pillow will be placed. Center of embroidery design should be approximately 15 inches (38cm) from center fold on sheet.

EMBROIDERY DIRECTIONS

To begin, "lock" ribbon onto needle by threading ribbon through eye of needle and inserting point of needle back through the short end about ⅜ inch (1cm) away from end. Pull the long length to "lock" ribbon onto needle. See page 15.

1. Roses: using 4mm tea rose, work one French knot (see page 16) in center. Fill in with a chain stitch (page 16), working outward from center in a spiral to desired size.

2. Stems: using 2mm moss, work all stems in a stem stitch (see page 16).

3. Leaves: using 4mm moss and spring moss, work all leaves in a lazy daisy stitch (see page 16), mixing colors as desired.

4. Purple flowers: using 4mm iris and grape, work flowers in 3 straight stitches. Use grape for 2 outside stitches and iris for center stitches.

5. Fan flowers: using ⅛-inch (3mm) double-face satin ribbon in dusty rose and apricot, make 2 fan flowers of each color for each pillowcase and 4 of each color for sheet. To make fan flower, cut 12 inches (30.5cm) of ribbon and mark every inch (2.5cm). With a threaded needle, start at one end and take a small stitch at each interval for entire length. Pull thread tightly. Take several stitches through all thicknesses to hold. Knot off. Attach to embroidery with 1 lazy daisy stitch with 4mm Silk-Ease emroidery ribbon in center and 1 straight stitch on each side to create a calyx and secure flower to background. Place colors randomly.

Embroidered Victorian Linens

Enlarge to 133%

Ribbon Embroidered Duvet

Enlarge to 230%

Embroidered Victorian Linens, Ribbon Embroidered Duvet

Ribbon Embroidered Duvet

Soft, easy-care ribbons and familiar embroidery stitches breathe new life into this charming old craft.

RIBBON

- 1 package of 2mm Silk-Ease embroidery ribbon in moss
- 2 packages of 4mm Silk-Ease embroidery ribbon in moss
- 1 package each of 4mm Silk-Ease ribbon in colonial rose, spring moss, iris, and grape
- 2 yards (2m) each of ⅛-inch-wide (3mm) double-face satin ribbon in peach and wild rose
- 4½ yards (4m) of 2¼-inch-wide (5.5cm) light pink single-face satin ribbon
- 8 yards (7.5m) of ⅛-inch-wide (3mm) peach mini-dot double-face satin ribbon
- 2⅝ yards (2.5m) of 1½-inch-wide (4cm) peach sheer satin stripe ribbon

OTHER MATERIALS

- Purchased duvet cover with Battenburg lace details
- Invisible thread and matching thread
- Embroidery and chenille needles
- Disappearing ink marker

INSTRUCTIONS

1. Cut 2¼-inch-wide (5.5cm) light pink ribbon into 2 equal lengths. Mark center of each length.

2. With marker, transfer design on page 52 to the ribbon. Align center marks on the pattern with the center of ribbon lengths.

3. Work embroidery following the directions on page 52. Remove any markings and press.

4. Arrange ribbons on duvet cover to fit design. Miter corners. Stitch miters in place.

5. Pin ribbon to duvet. Topstitch in place, using invisible thread in needle and regular thread in bobbin.

6. Using lengths of ⅛-inch-wide (3mm) mini-dot ribbon, outline all edges of 2¼-inch-wide (5.5cm) light pink ribbon. Topstitch in place with a narrow zigzag stitch.

7. Cut sheer satin stripe into 4 equal lengths. Tie a bow with each length; tack to mitered corners.

Magnolia Centerpiece, Rose Napkin Rings

Magnolia Centerpiece

Make an oversized basket filled with flowers and gorgeous ribbons into an elegant centerpiece for any special occasion.

RIBBON

- 8¼ yards (7.5m) of 1½-inch-wide (4cm) burgundy sheer wire-edge ribbon
- 6¾ yards (6.5m) of 2½-inch-wide (6.5cm) floral tapestry ribbon

OTHER MATERIALS

- Gold planter
- Floral foam to fit base
- 6 purchased silk magnolia flowers and buds
- Assorted evergreen sprays and fruit picks
- 12 gold pussy willow branches
- Sheet moss
- Floral wire
- Low-temperature glue gun and glue sticks

INSTRUCTIONS

1. From burgundy ribbon, cut eight 22-inch (56cm) lengths. Make 8 gathered roses as instructed on page 22. Secure on wires and set aside.

2. From remaining sheer ribbon, cut two 24-inch (61cm) lengths and two 36-inch (1m) lengths. Form streamers by folding ribbon lengths in half and securing at fold on wire. Cut all ends to form a V. Set aside.

3. From 2½-inch-wide (6.5cm) floral tapestry ribbon, cut four 36-inch (1m) lengths and four 48-inch (1.5m) lengths. Make 2 four-loop bows and 2 two-loop bows with 8-inch (20.5cm) tails from the 4 shorter lengths of ribbon. See page 17 for instructions. With longer lengths, make 4 sets of streamers by folding lengths in half and securing fold to wire. Cut all ends to form a V.

4. Cut floral foam to fit in planter base. Glue to secure.

5. Using photograph on previous page as a guide, insert silk magnolias into floral foam. Add ribbon bows and ribbon roses. Follow with evergreen sprays, fruit picks, and streamers. Finish the centerpiece by adding gold pussy willow branches.

Rose Napkin Rings

A perfect accent to your Magnolia Centerpiece, these napkin rings will beautify your dinner table.

RIBBON

Ring A

- 1½ yards (1.5m) of 1½-inch-wide (4cm) sheer burgundy wire-edge ribbon
- ¼ yard (23cm) of 2½-inch (6.5cm) floral tapestry wire-edge ribbon

Ring B

- ¾ yard (69cm) of ⅝-inch-wide (1.5cm) metallic novelty ribbon
- ½ yard (45.5cm) of 2½-inch-wide (6.5cm) floral tapestry ribbon

OTHER MATERIALS

- Old napkin ring to cover or toilet paper roll cut into 2-inch (5cm) lengths
- Hot glue gun and glue sticks

INSTRUCTIONS

1. For ring A, cut a 27-inch (68.5cm) length of burgundy ribbon. Wrap ribbon around napkin ring. Glue to secure. Fold 2½-inch-wide (6.5cm) ribbon so wire edges are hidden. Wrap length around covered napkin ring and glue in place. Make one fancy rose as instructed on page 21. Glue rose onto ring, covering seam.

2. For ring B, wrap metallic novelty ribbon around napkin ring. Fold tapestry ribbon to fit in center of napkin ring with finished edges showing. Seam ends together. With remaining tapestry ribbon, make a bow with center knot. Glue bow on ring, covering seam.

3. Ring may be further embellished with fruit, leaves, and other items.

Tea Time Table Set

Blue and white country prints accented with ribbon trims recall the fragrances of grandma's kitchen.

RIBBON

- 1⅝ (1.5m) yards of 1½-inch-wide (4cm) jacquard ribbon for each place mat
- ⅜ yard (34.5cm) of 1½-inch-wide (4cm) jacquard ribbon for each napkin ring
- 1 yard (1m) of 1½-inch-wide (4cm) jacquard ribbon for tea cozy

FABRIC

- Place mat: 1 yard (1m) yields 3 place mats
- Table runner: length of table plus 27 inches (68.5cm)
- Tea cozy: ¾ yard (69cm)
- Napkin: ¼ yard (69cm) yields 6 napkins
- Napkin ring: made from fabric scraps; ⅜ yard (34.5cm) yields about a dozen

OTHER MATERIALS

- Matching thread
- Batting
- Purchased piping for place mats, table runner, and tea cozy
- Purchased or self-made binding for napkins

INSTRUCTIONS

1. For place mats, table runner, and tea cozy, make paper patterns as shown in diagram on page 59.

2. Cut fabric from patterns as follows: 2 for each place mat, 2 for table runner, and 4 for tea cozy. Cut batting as follows: one for each place mat, one for table runner, and 2 for tea cozy.

3. Baste batting to wrong side of corresponding fabric pieces for place mats, table runner, and tea cozy.

4. With zipper foot, stitch piping to outside edges of each place mat, table runner, and one side only of tea cozy, aligning raw edges and using a ½-inch (1.5cm) seam. Begin place mat and table runner at concave corner, tucking ends in neatly. Clip piping seam allowance deeply at each corner as you sew. Handstitch to join if necessary. On tea cozy, begin on lower left side, and stitch up and across, ending on lower right and leaving bottom edge free of piping.

5. For place mats and table runner, stitch back to front with right sides together, leaving an opening for turning. Turn. Slipstitch opening closed. Beginning in one corner, apply ribbon ¼ inch (6mm) inside edges. Stitch ribbon along both edges, folding ribbon excess under at each corner and mitering the corners. Fold ends under at beginning and end, hiding ends in a miter.

6. For tea cozy, apply ribbon only on front as described in previous step. Stitch front to back along sides and upper edge. Stitch tea cozy lining front to lining back along sides and upper edge. With right sides together, stitch tea cozy to tea cozy lining along lower edge. Leave an opening for turning. Turn right side out and slipstitch opening closed.

7. Napkins are 14-inch (35.5cm) squares and napkin rings are 3-by-10 inch (7.5 by 25.5cm) bias strips. Cut one fabric piece for each napkin and napkin ring.

8. Encase raw edges of napkin in binding, mitering at corners and overlapping ends. Stitch in place.

9. Press both long edges of fabric strip for napkin ring under ½ inch (1.5cm). Center ribbon on fabric strip, covering raw edges of fabric. Stitch ribbon in place along each edge. Seam ends, right sides together, to form a ring.

10. Fold ring at seam line, ribbon sides together, and push to the side at a 45-degree angle to form miter across ribbon. Tack in place.

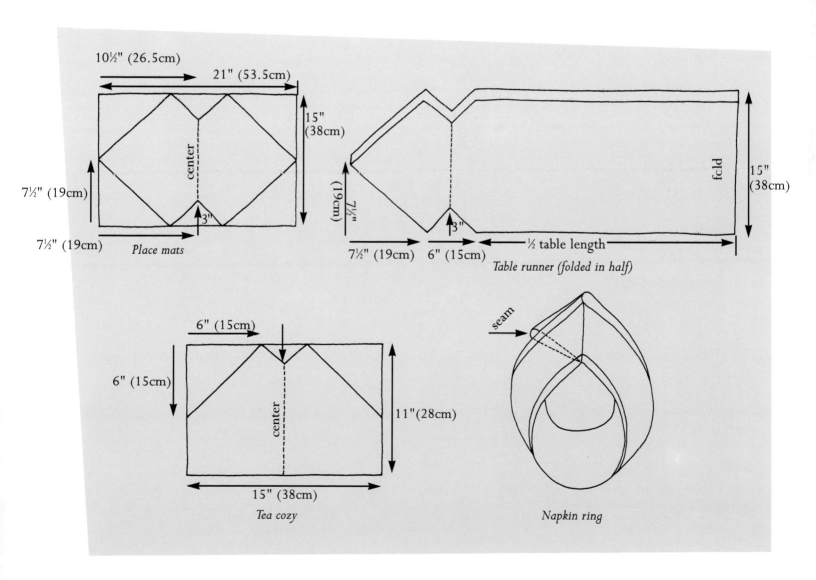

Sweet Pea Lamp and Shade

A colorful garden of ribbon sweet peas doesn't need watering to look fresh and pretty day after day on this charming lamp and shade.

RIBBON

- ¾ yard (69cm) each of 1½-inch-wide (4cm) red and pink ombre wire-edge ribbon
- 4½ yards (4.5m) of 1½-inch-wide (4cm) purple ombre wire-edge ribbon
- 4¾ yards (4.5m) of ⅝-inch-wide (1.5cm) green ombre wire-edge ribbon

OTHER MATERIALS

- Candlestick lamp and shade
- 1½-inch-thick (4cm) floral foam square to cover lamp base
- Sheet moss
- 24-gauge green-covered wire and stem wire
- Green floral tape
- Low-temperature glue gun and glue sticks
- Size 4 or 5 knitting needle

INSTRUCTIONS

1. Cut all 1½-inch-wide (4cm) ribbon into 7-inch (18cm) lengths. Mark each length for 3 petals, one 3-inch (7.5cm) petal and two 2-inch (5cm) petals. Make 23 sweet peas as instructed on page 25. For variety, use both sides of colored edges on ombre ribbons.

2. Cut green ombre ribbon into 6-inch (15cm) lengths. Make 28 pulled leaves as instructed on page 19.

3. Cut 15 lengths each 4 to 6 inches (10 to 15cm) of 24-gauge covered wire. Wrap tightly around knitting needle. Pull coiled wire open to make curly tendrils and slip off needle.

4. To form branches, randomly attach flowers, leaves, and tendrils to a length of stem wire. Wrap with floral tape. For the lamp base, use 2 branches containing 9 assorted flowers, 15 leaves, and 6 tendrils. For lamp shade, use 2 branches containing the 14 remaining flowers, 13 leaves, and 9 tendrils.

5. Cut floral foam to fit base of lamp. Glue to base. Cover with sheet moss and secure in place.

6. Insert first two branches into base. Glue to secure. Gently bend and shape sweet pea vines to encircle lamp. Glue vines to lamp base as needed to hold vines upright.

7. Arrange 2 remaining branches on lamp shade as shown in photograph on next page.

CAUTION: To prevent danger of fire, do not secure any vines inside lamp shade or near bulb.

Rose Garland on a Chain

Lush ribbon roses and buds linked together to form a lifelike rose garland will enhance anything you drape it over.

RIBBON

- 1½-inch-wide (4cm) taffeta wire-edge ribbon for all flowers; amount depends on length of garland and number of flowers desired
- 15-inch (38cm) length of ribbon for each small rosebud
- 25-inch (63.5cm) length of ribbon for each medium rosebud
- 40-inch (1m) length of ribbon for each rose
- 6-inch (15cm) length of ⅝-inch-wide (1.5cm) green ombre wire-edge ribbon for each leaf

NOTE: For variety, use both sides of colored edges on ombre ribbon. Also, consider adding other flowers of your choice.

OTHER MATERIALS

- 6-foot (2m) lamp chain for swag, cut to desired length
- 24-gauge green-covered wire
- Stamens
- Size 5 or 6 knitting needle

INSTRUCTIONS

1. Referring to photograph on the next page for suggested placement, weave stem wire through chain links. Wrap wire around links an extra time to keep vine from shifting.

2. Cut all 1½-inch (4cm) ribbon into 5-inch (13cm) lengths. Make rolled petals and assemble roses as instructed on page 20.

3. Cut ⅝-inch-wide (1.5cm) green ombre wire-edge ribbon into 6-inch (15cm) lengths. Make pulled leaves as instructed on page 19. Assemble leaf stems in combinations of 2 or 3. Use remaining leaves separately.

4. Cut 24-gauge wire into 4- to 6-inch (10 to 15cm) lengths. Wrap wire tightly around knitting needle. Remove and pull curly tendrils to open.

5. Using photograph on the next page as a guide, attach roses, buds, leaves, and tendrils randomly to vine. Vary the size and color of the roses. When finished, bend and shape roses, leaves, and tendrils into a pleasing arrangement.

CHAPTER THREE

Bridal Splendor

"There are ribbons in the sky for our love..."

—Stevie Wonder

Wedding Heart Box

Create this ribbon-trimmed heart-shaped box to save cherished mementos from your wedding day.

R I B B O N

- 3 yards (3m) of ⅜-inch-wide (1cm) white floral ribbon
- 1¼ yards (1m) of 1-inch-wide (2.5cm) white gathered-lace ribbon
- 1½ yards (1.5m) of ⅜-inch-wide (1cm) scalloped-edge white satin stripe ribbon
- 2 yards (2m) of ⅝-inch-wide (1.5cm) white jacquard ribbon
- 1 large, white, purchased satin rose

O T H E R   M A T E R I A L S

- Papier mâché heart box, approximately 7 by 3½ inches (18 by 9cm)
- Craft glue
- ¼ yard (23cm) of fabric for inside lid. Use lid insert to trace and cut heart shape.
- Fabric protector spray

NOTE: To allow for finishing edges, cut ribbon ½ inch (1.5cm) longer than area to be covered.

I N S T R U C T I O N S

1. Lift out lid insert. Brush glue on surface to be covered. Cut strips of ⅜-inch-wide (1cm) floral ribbon and ⅜-inch-wide (1cm) scalloped-edge ribbons to length needed. Alternate floral ribbon and scalloped-edge ribbons across heart insert. Wrap ends of ribbon to back side of shape, and glue in place. Press ribbons firmly with finger to ensure adhesion.

2. Glue strip of 1-inch (2.5cm) gathered-lace ribbon to side and then top of lid. Fold ends under for a neat finish.

3. If desired, glue heart-shaped fabric to back side of lid insert. Replace insert in lid.

4. Brush glue onto side edges of heart base. Starting at lower edge, alternate ⅝-inch-wide (1.5cm) jacquard and ⅜-inch-wide (1cm) floral ribbon until base is covered. Turn under raw ends.

5. Spray with fabric protector.

6. Glue purchased satin rose to center heart point on lid.

Photo Storage Box

Photos from your most memorable day can be stored in style in this lovely ribbon-embellished box.

RIBBON

- 3 yards (3m) of 1½-inch-wide (4cm) white grosgrain ribbon

- 1⅛ yards (1m) of 1-inch-wide (2.5cm) white novelty lace ribbon

- 1¾ yards (1.5m) of ⅞-inch-wide (2cm) white novelty ribbon

- 4 yards (3.5m) of ⅜ inch wide (1cm) white floral ribbon

- 2⅛ (2m) yards of ⅞-inch-wide (1cm) lace-edge satin ribbon

OTHER MATERIALS

- White photo storage box, 7¾ by 11¼ inches (19.5 by 28.5cm), painted if necessary

- Craft glue

- Fabric protector spray

INSTRUCTIONS

1. Measure and cut strips of ribbons ½ inch (1.5cm) longer than needed. Brush glue on surface to be covered. Place ribbon strips vertically on lid, starting with grosgrain ribbon and following with floral ribbon, novelty ribbon, and floral ribbon again. Repeat this pattern until lid is covered. Wrap ¼ inch (6mm) of both ends of ribbon over side edges and glue in place. Press all ribbons firmly with finger to ensure adhesion. Center strips of lace-edge satin ribbon over strips of 1½-inch-wide (4cm) grosgrain ribbon and glue in place.

2. Glue strips of floral ribbon to upper and lower edges around all 4 sides of lid. Center novelty lace ribbon between rows of floral ribbon and glue in place. Fold edges under for a neat finish.

3. Brush glue onto side edges of box base. Starting at lower edge, place a strip of grosgrain, a strip of novelty ribbon, and another strip of grosgrain ribbon. Layer a strip of floral ribbon at lower edge of box on top of grosgrain ribbon. Glue in place. Center a strip of lace-edge satin ribbon on remaining space of lower grosgrain ribbon and glue in place. Turn under ¼ inch (6mm) to hide all raw ends.

4. Paint or line inside of box if desired.

5. Spray with fabric protector.

Small Square Box

Elegant satin and taffeta ribbons make an ordinary box a perfect keepsake for your bridal attendants.

RIBBON

- 1⅛ yards (1m) of 1½-inch-wide (4cm) white and gold novelty ribbon
- 2⅛ yards (2m) of ⅜-inch-wide (1cm) white and gold novelty ribbon

OTHER MATERIALS

- Small box, 5¼ by 5¼ inches (13 by 13cm)
- Craft glue
- Fabric protector spray

INSTRUCTIONS

1. Measure and cut strips of ribbons ½ inch (1.5cm) longer than needed. Brush glue on surface to be covered. Alternate both ribbons across top of box lid. Wrap ¼-inch (6mm) end of ribbon to side of lid and glue in place. Press ribbons firmly with finger to ensure adhesion.

2. Glue 2 strips of narrow ribbon around sides of lid. Fold ends under for a neat finish.

3. Brush glue onto sides of box base. Starting at lower edge, alternate both ribbons until base is covered. Turn under ¼ inch (6mm) to hide raw ends.

4. Paint or line inside of box if desired.

5. Spray with fabric protector.

Small Square Box, Photo Storage Box, Wedding Heart Box, Wedding Frame

Wedding Frame

Your wedding invitation can be lovingly displayed for years to come in this ribbon rose-trimmed picture frame.

RIBBON

- 1 large white purchased satin rose
- 17 small white purchased roses with white leaves

OTHER MATERIALS

- 8-by-10-inch (20.5 by 25.5cm) frame
- Oval mat for frame with 5-by-7-inch (13 by 18cm) opening
- ½ yard (45.5cm) of white, rose-patterned damask fabric
- Craft glue

INSTRUCTIONS

1. Using oval mat as pattern, trace opening and edges on wrong side of fabric. Mark ½-inch (1.5cm) allowances, and use this mark as your cutting line. Clip curves around oval opening, being careful to stop ⅛ inch (3mm) from actual curve marking.

2. Coat surface of mat with glue. Place wrong side of fabric to mat, aligning all markings. Smooth fabric and press to adhere. Smooth corners and edges of oval. Press raw edges to back side and glue in place one side at a time.

3. Glue large satin rose at the center lower edge of oval opening. Glue small roses all around oval opening.

4. Replace mat in frame.

Ring Bearer's Pillow

Elaborate ribbon weaving is used to create this heirloom ring bearer's pillow.

RIBBON

- 5½ yards (5m) of ⅝-inch-wide (1.5cm) white satin ribbon (ribbon A)
- 5½ yards (5m) of ⅝-inch-wide (1.5cm) white floral ribbon (ribbon B)
- 6½ yards (6m) of ⅝-inch-wide (1.5cm) gold-edge ribbon (ribbon C)
- 2 yards (2m) of 1½-inch-wide (4cm) gold-trim wire-edge ribbon
- 1 yard (1m) of ⅞-inch-wide (2cm) sheer gold ribbon

OTHER MATERIALS

- 11-by-14-inch (28 by 35.5cm) piece of fusible interfacing
- 10-inch (25.5cm) square of white satin fabric
- 2 squares of muslin, 10 inches (25.5cm) each
- Matching thread
- Fiberfil

NOTE: Seam allowance is ½ inch (1.5cm).

INSTRUCTIONS

1. Cut fourteen 14-inch (35.5cm) lengths of ribbon A for warp ribbons. Weave 19 rows with ribbon B for first set of diagonal ribbons as instructed on pages 27–28. Weave 19 rows with ribbon C for second set of diagonal ribbons. A tumbling blocks pattern will be formed. Fuse ribbons to interfacing.

2. Stitch around weaving and trim excess. With right sides together, stitch satin square to weaving, leaving opening. Trim seam and turn.

3. Right sides together, stitch muslin squares together for pillow liner. Turn and lightly stuff with Fiberfil. Insert liner into pillow and slipstitch opening closed.

4. Carefully pull wire along one edge of gold-trimmed ribbon edge to gather for ruffle. Slipstitch gathered ribbon around edge of pillow. Stitch ribbon together at ends.

5. As instructed on page 17, make a four-loop bow with sheer gold and white satin ribbon. With remaining ribbon C, create a two-loop bow with long streamers, and slipstitch it to the center of the first bow. Stitch completed bow to pillow. Tie rings onto ends of ribbon streamers.

Guest Book

Wedding guests can record their names and best wishes in this gorgeous guest book.

RIBBON

- 5 yards (4.5m) of ⅝-inch-wide (1.5cm) white satin ribbon (ribbon A)
- 4¾ yards (4.5m) of ⅝-inch-wide (1.5cm) white floral ribbon (ribbon B)
- 4¾ yards (4.5m) of ⅝-inch-wide (1.5cm) sheer stripe ribbon (ribbon C)
- ⅝ yard (57.5cm) of 1½-inch-wide (4cm) gold-edge sheer ribbon
- ½ yard (45.5cm) of 1½-inch-wide (4cm) white wire-edge ribbon
- ½ yard (45.5cm) of 1½-inch-wide (4cm) gold ribbon
- 1½ yards (1.5m) of ¼-inch (6mm) ivory cording

OTHER MATERIALS

- 10-inch (25.5cm) square of fusible interfacing
- 8-by-10-inch (20.5 by 25.5cm) piece of white satin fabric
- Matching thread
- 6¼-by-8¼-inch (16 by 21cm) bridal guest book
- 6¼-by-17-inch (16 by 43cm) poster board
- Craft glue

Key to My Heart Sachet Pillow, Ring Bearer's Pillow, Guest Book

INSTRUCTIONS

1. Cut a 10-inch (25.5cm) square of fusible interfacing and place adhesive side up. Cut 15 lengths, each 12 inches (30.5cm), of ribbon A for warp (vertical) ribbons. Weave 16 rows of ribbon B for first set of diagonal ribbons as instructed on page 28. Weave 16 rows of ribbon C for second set. A tumbling blocks pattern will be formed. Fuse ribbons to interfacing. Stitch around weaving and trim excess.

2. With right sides together, stitch one 8-inch (20.5cm) side of satin fabric to one 10-inch (25.5cm) side of weaving. Satin fabric will be on the back of the guest book.

3. Bend poster board around guest book. Glue weaving and satin to the poster board. Raw edges are glued to the back of the poster board. Make sure the fabric is not so tight that the bent board won't fit over the guest book.

4. Glue covered poster board to the front and back of the guest book.

5. Glue cording around all edges of the guest book.

6. With sheer gold-edged ribbon, make a two-loop bow as instructed on page 17, and glue it to the front of the book. With 1½-inch-wide (4cm) white wire-edge ribbon, make a gathered rose as instructed on page 22, and glue it to the center of the bow. Cut the 1½-inch-wide (4cm) gold sheer ribbon in half and make 2 gathered leaves as instructed on page 21. Glue leaves around rose.

Key to My Heart Sachet Pillow

This heart-shaped pillow woven with satin and floral ribbon and filled with delicately scented potpourri will evoke memories of your wedding day.

RIBBON

- 5½ yards (5m) of ⅜-inch-wide (1cm) white satin ribbon (ribbon A)
- 5½ yards (5m) of ⅜-inch-wide (1cm) cream satin ribbon (ribbon B)
- 5½ yards (5m) of ⅜-inch-wide (1cm) white floral ribbon (ribbon C)
- 1½ yards (1.5m) of ⅛-inch-wide (3mm) white satin double-face ribbon
- ½ yard (45.5cm) of ⅜-inch-wide (1cm) sheer novelty ribbon
- ½ yard (45.5cm) of ⅞-inch-wide (2cm) sheer white and gold ribbon
- ⅜ yard (30.5cm) of ⅞-inch-wide (2cm) white taffeta wire-edge ribbon

OTHER MATERIALS

- 9-inch (23cm) square of fusible interfacing
- 9-inch (23cm) square of satin fabric
- Matching thread
- Gold key charm
- Fiberfil
- Potpourri
- Craft glue

NOTE: Seam allowance is ½ inch (1.5cm).

INSTRUCTIONS

1. Alternating ribbons A, B, and C, cut 22 lengths, each 9 inches (23cm), for warp. Lay interfacing with adhesive side up. Alternate ribbons in above manner and weave 22 rows for the first set of diagonal ribbons as instructed on page 28. Ribbon A should go under warp A and C, and over B; ribbon B should go over ribbons A and B, and under C; ribbon C should go under ribbons B and C, and over A. Alternating ribbons to create hexagonal shapes, weave 22 rows of ribbon for the second set of diagonals. Fuse ribbons to interfacing.

2. Trace pattern on following page onto weaving and stitch along cutting edge. Cut out heart close to stitching. Cut heart shape from satin.

3. Baste ⅜-inch-wide (1cm) sheer novelty ribbon to the top edges of the heart to form a hanger loop. With right sides together, stitch pillow, leaving an opening for turning. Trim and turn. Stuff lightly with Fiberfil and potpourri. Slipstitch opening closed.

4. Make a two-loop bow with ⅞-inch-wide (2cm) sheer white and gold ribbon. Thread charm onto ⅛-inch-wide (3mm) satin ribbon and form a florist bow, letting one loop hang longer with the key charm. See instructions on page 17. Wire onto first bow. Glue to center of heart.

5. From taffeta wire-edge ribbon, make a gathered rose as instructed on page 22. Glue to center of bow.

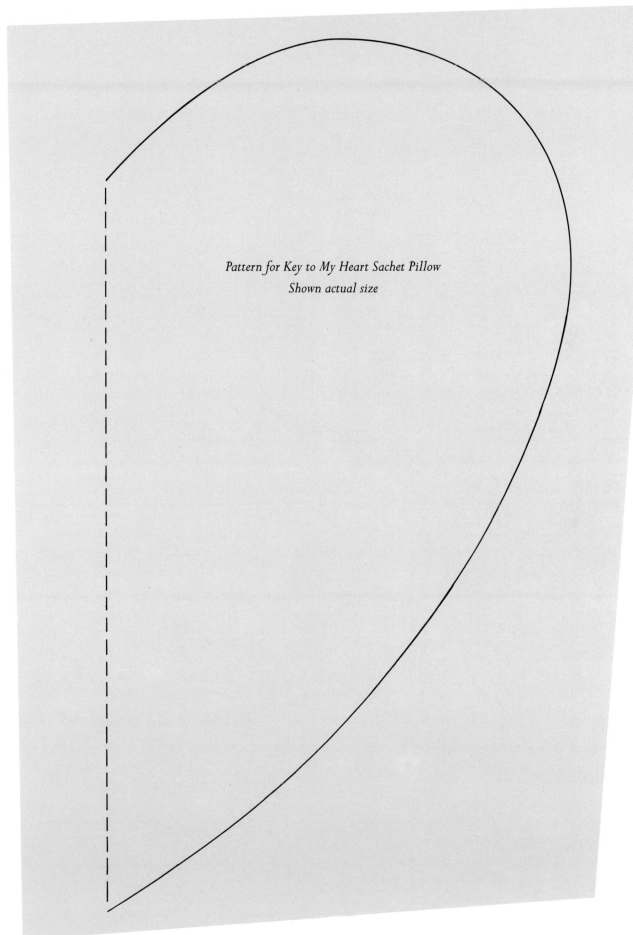

Pattern for Key to My Heart Sachet Pillow
Shown actual size

🌀

Bridal Topiary

*Create a very special bridal shower centerpiece with pink and white ribbon roses and pretty
sheer ribbon streamers added to a double ball topiary.*

RIBBON

- 5½ yards (5m) of ⅞-inch-wide (2cm) pink sheer wire-edge ribbon
- 2 yards (2m) of ⅞-inch-wide (2cm) white sheer wire-edge ribbon
- 1¾ yards (1.5m) of 1½-inch-wide (4cm) white sheer wire-edge ribbon
- 4 yards (4m) of 1½-inch-wide (4cm) pink wire-edge ribbon
- 4 yards (4m) of 1½ to 2-inch-wide (4cm) wire-edge ribbon
- 3½ yards (3.5m) of 1½-inch-wide (4cm) green ombre wire-edge ribbon
- 2 yards (2m) of ⅞-inch-wide (2cm) pink ombre wire-edge ribbon
- 1 yard (1m) of ⅝-inch-wide (1.5cm) green wire-edge ribbon

OTHER MATERIALS

- 1 double ball topiary form
- 1 urn or basket to fit base of form
- 48 white pearl stamens
- U-pins
- Sheet moss
- White sparkle gypsophila
- Hot glue gun and glue sticks

INSTRUCTIONS

1. Glue moss to topiary balls and base. Glue topiary into urn or basket. Cut a 27-inch (68.5cm) length of pink sheer ribbon. Beginning at base of topiary ball, wrap stem. Pin at bottom of lower topiary ball. Bring ribbon to top of ball and pin. Wrap upper stem and pin to base of upper ball. Let streamer hang.

2. Holding 2 yards (2m) of ⅞-inch-wide (2cm) pink and white sheer ribbons together, make a florist bow with a set of short and long streamers. See page 17 for directions. Pin bow to top of upper ball. Bring short streamers to bottom of upper ball and pin, shaping as desired. Bring long streamers to top of lower ball and pin. Pin again at bottom of lower ball, shaping as desired.

3. With 1½-inch-wide (4cm) white sheer wire-edge ribbon, make a six-loop bow. With 1¼ yards (1m) of pink sheer ribbon, make an eight-loop bow and wire to the center of larger bow. See page 17 for instructions to make these bows. Glue bow to top of lower ball. Tie remaining pink sheer ribbon around urn or basket. Cut streamers on diagonal.

4. Cut 1½-inch-wide (4cm) white ribbon into 24-inch (61cm) lengths and make 6 large gathered roses as instructed on page 22. Cut 1½-inch-wide (4cm) pink ribbon into 18-inch (45.5cm) lengths and make

8 morning glories, using 6 stamens for centers. See page 24 for directions. Cut 1½-inch-wide (4cm) green ribbon into 9-inch (23cm) lengths and make 14 large gathered leaves as instructed on page 21. Cut ⅞-inch-wide (2cm) pink ribbon into 12-inch (30.5cm) lengths and make 6 small gathered roses. Cut ⅝-inch-wide (1.5cm) green ribbon into 6-inch (15cm) lengths and make 6 small gathered leaves. Glue flowers, leaves, and small bunches of gypsophila to the topiary balls.

Bridal Chair Back Swag

This chair swag is the perfect accent to the bride's "guest of honor" seat at her bridal shower.

RIBBON

- 5½ yards (5m) of 1½-inch-wide (4cm) sheer pink wire-edge ribbon
- 3 yards (3m) of ⅞-inch-wide (2cm) sheer pink wire-edge ribbon
- 2⅓ yards (2m) of 1½-inch-wide (4cm) white wire-edge ribbon
- 2 yards (2m) of 1½-inch-wide (4cm) pink wire-edge ribbon
- 2 yards (2m) of 1½-inch-wide (4cm) green ombre wire-edge ribbon
- 1¼ yards (1m) of ⅝-inch-wide (1.5cm) sheer pink ribbon

OTHER MATERIALS

- 24 white pearl stamens
- Eucalyptus
- Sparkle gypsophila
- Paddle wire
- Low-temperature glue gun and glue sticks

INSTRUCTIONS

1. Cut a 56-inch (1.5m) length of 1½-inch-wide (4cm) sheer pink wire-edge ribbon for base of swag. Beginning about 15 inches (38cm) from one end, wire small bunches of eucalyptus and gypsophila to the ribbon. Continue to wire florals onto the ribbon, overlapping stems to create a full swag. Ends of ribbon hang as streamers. The swag should be made long enough to fit back of your chair.

2. Cut ⅞-inch-wide (2cm) sheer pink wire-edge ribbon in half. Fold each length in half and wire onto the ends of the swag for ties. Cut remaining 1½-inch-wide (4cm) sheer pink wire-edge ribbon in half. From each length, make a four-loop bow with center loop as directed on page 17. Wire a bow to each end of swag. Trim all streamers on diagonal.

3. Cut 1½-inch-wide (4cm) green wire-edge ribbon into eight 9-inch (23cm) lengths. From each length, make a gathered leaf as instructed on page 21. From 1½-inch-wide (4cm) pink wire-edge ribbon, cut four 18-inch

(45.5cm) lengths and make morning glories as instructed on page 24, using 6 stamens for flower centers. Cut two 24-inch (61cm) lengths and three 12-inch (30.5cm) lengths of 1½-inch-wide (4cm) white wire-edge ribbon, and make 2 large and 3 small gathered roses as instructed on page 22.

4. Glue all flowers and leaves to the swag. Loop and glue ⅝-inch-wide (1.5cm) sheer ribbon through the swag.

5. Additional roses and leaves may be made to decorate small purchased boxes to be given as favors.

Bridal Headpiece and Veil

A beautiful ribbon headpiece will be the crowning glory of a bride's wedding ensemble.

RIBBON

- 9 yards (8.5m) of ⅝-inch-wide (1.5cm) cream feather-edge double-face satin ribbon
- 8 yards (7.5m) of ⅝-inch-wide (1.5cm) cream wire-edge ribbon

OTHER MATERIALS

- 3 yards bridal veiling
- Matching thread
- 14 pearl stamens
- 18 pearl stamens and sprays
- ¾ yard (69cm) of strung pearls
- 18-gauge wire and fine floral wire
- White floral tape
- Craft glue

INSTRUCTIONS

1. Cut all ⅝-inch-wide (1.5cm) wire-edge ribbon into 4-inch (10cm) lengths. Make all lengths into pulled leaf, petals as instructed on page 19.

2. Wire 5 petals around 1 pearl stamen, overlapping petals. Secure all petals and cover raw edges with white floral tape. Make 14 flowers. Set aside.

3. Assemble 18 pearl stamens and sprays into 4 branches: 2 with 4 stamens and 2 branches with 5 stamens. Set aside.

4. Using several thicknesses of 18-gauge wire, form circlet to fit head, approximately 22 to 24 inches (56 to 61cm). Cover with white floral tape.

5. Glue pearls to center 4 inches (10cm) of circlet. Compress pearls tightly to cover wire.

6. Using the photograph on the next page as a guide, attach 7 flowers, one 4-stamen branch, and one 5-stamen branch to each side of circlet with floral tape.

7. From feather edge ribbon, cut two 30-inch (76cm) lengths, four 36-inch (1m) lengths, and two 58-inch (1.5m) lengths. From 58-inch (1.5m) lengths, make 2 six-loop bows (see page 17) with 11-inch (28cm) streamers. Secure with wire. Add one 30-inch (76cm) length and one 36-inch (91cm) length to both bows. Glue to circlet at end of flowers. Tie onto circlet with remaining 36-inch (91cm) length. Cut all ends to form a V.

8. Following the diagram on page 82, mark veiling in 30 inches (76cm) from one edge. Mark in 45 inches (114cm) from same edge. Gather veiling across width, first at 30-inch (76cm) marking then at 45-inch (114cm) marking. Pull up both gathered areas to measure 4 inches (10cm) and secure. Sew 2 rows of gathering stitches together to form pouf. Round off all corners to finish. Attach to back of circlet.

Bridal Headpiece and Veil, Bridesmaid Headpiece

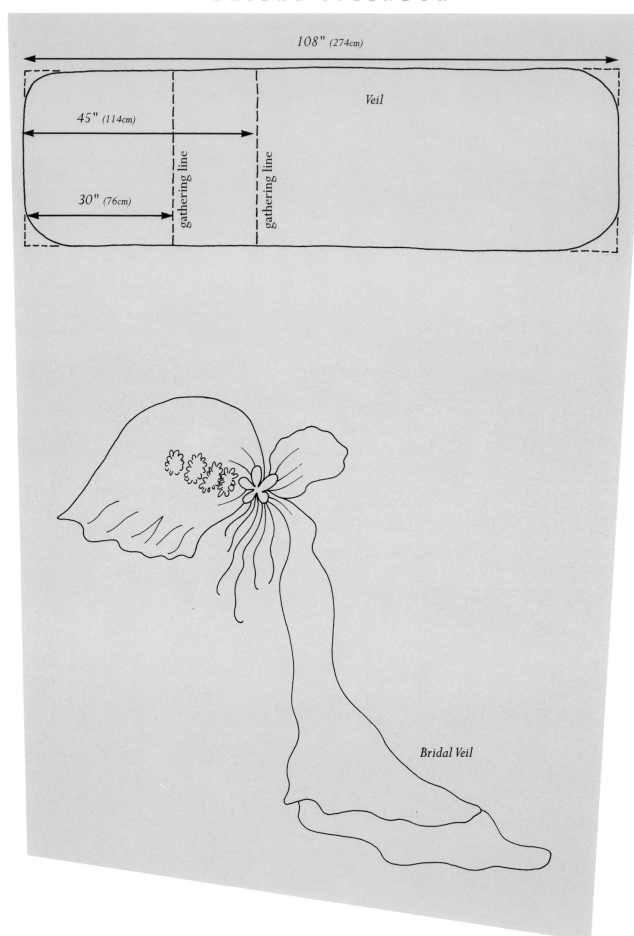

108" (274cm)

Veil

45" (114cm)

30" (76cm)

gathering line

gathering line

Bridal Veil

Bridesmaid Headpiece

*A perfect complement to the bride's headpiece, a garland of ribbon flowers creates a
delicate wreath to encircle the heads of bridesmaids and flower girls.*

Follow instructions for Bridal Headpiece on page 80, but eliminate veiling and replace with ribbon bows in back. (See picture on page 81 for reference.) Divide 8 yards (7.5m) of ⅝-inch-wide (1.5cm) wire-edge ribbon into the number of flower colors to be used in the headpiece. Replace 18 pearl stamens and sprays with green leaves made from ⅝-inch-wide (1.5cm) green ombre wire-edge ribbon in pulled leaf style. See directions on page 19. Wire on stems and insert as desired.

Wedding Nosegay

*Make this Victorian-inspired nosegay to give the bride as a special keepsake
from her bridal shower or engagement party.*

RIBBON

- 1 yard (1m) of ⅞-inch-wide (2cm) sheer and pearls ribbon
- 1 yard (1m) of ⅜-inch-wide (1cm) taffeta and pearls ribbon
- 1 yard (1m) each ⅜-inch-wide (1cm) feather-edge double-face satin ribbon in white and green
- 1 yard (1m) of ⅛-inch-wide (3mm) double-face satin ribbon
- 1 yard (1m) of ⅝-inch-wide (1.5cm) double-face satin ribbon
- 3 yards (3m) of 1½-inch-wide (4cm) double-face satin ribbon
- 5½ yards (5m) of 1½-inch-wide (4cm) white wire-edge ribbon
- 1 yard (1m) of 1½-inch-wide (4cm) sheer stripe feather-edge ribbon
- 15 purchased ribbon roses with green leaves
- 27 purchased lace cockades

OTHER MATERIALS

- 24-gauge wire (cut into 10" [25.5cm] lengths)
- Florist tape and wire

INSTRUCTIONS

1. Cut ⅞-inch (2cm) sheer and pearl center ribbon into 2½-inch (6.5cm) lengths. Fold lengths in half lengthwise. Twist ends with wire to make loop.

2. Insert wire through ribbon roses between leaf and flower, twisting to hold in place. Repeat with lace cockades. Set aside.

3. Cut 1½-inch-wide (4cm) wire-edge ribbon into five 22-inch (56cm) lengths and five 18-inch (45.5cm) lengths. From the 22-inch (56cm) lengths, and following the directions on page 22, make 5 gathered roses. From the 18-inch (45.5cm) lengths, make 5 fancy roses. (See page 21). Wire to stem and cover with florist tape.

4. For nosegay, hold one fancy rose at top center, carefully placing 3 or more lace cockades evenly around center rose. Continuing to hold, add remaining 4 fancy roses around outer edges. Finish with 5 gathered roses. Place lace cockades, ribbon roses, and ribbon loops between roses to fill in spaces.

5. Shape as desired. Wire nosegay together. Trim wires and cover with florist tape. Cover tape with 1½-inch-wide (4cm) satin ribbon, ending at base of nosegay. Crisscross with green ribbon to achieve a braided effect. Tie remaining ribbons as streamers at base and cover with remaining 1½-inch-wide (4cm) satin ribbon. Finish with a bow made from 1½-inch-wide (4cm) sheer striped featheredge ribbon. Cut streamers in varying lengths.

Tea Bag Potpourri

These delightful ribbon tea bags provide a delicate potpourri fragrance
and will make treasured bridal shower mementos.

RIBBON

- 15 inches (38cm) of 2¼-inch-wide (5.5cm) sheer gold-edge ribbon
- ½ yard (45.5cm) of ⅛-inch-wide (3mm) double-face satin ribbon
- 1 purchased small satin rose

OTHER MATERIALS

- 2 tablespoons crushed potpourri

INSTRUCTIONS

1. Fold under ⅜-inch (1cm) hem on one end of 2¼-inch-wide (5.5cm) ribbon. Measure 5½ inches (14cm) down from hemmed edge and fold along this marking. Glue both sides together to form a 5½-inch (14cm) pocket. Distribute potpourri evenly in pocket.

2. To create a "flow-thru" look fold the 5½-inch (14cm) pocket in half, bringing original fold to front hemmed edge. Create an inverted pleat at new bottom fold. Glue back to front to completely seal opening. (See step 1.)

3. To create flap on tea bag, turn tea bag to back side. Fold raw edge to one back side edge, creating a triangle. (See step 2.) Glue in place. Fold top point down to opposite side, completing peaked flap. Glue in place, aligning all edges. (See step 3.)

4. Turn flap over sealed access and glue in place.

5. Following the directions on page 17, form a small two-loop bow with tails from ⅛-inch-wide (3mm) double-face satin ribbon. Trim tails.

6. Use remaining ⅛-inch-wide (3mm) double-face satin ribbon to form tea bag string and glue from tip of flap to fold. Glue bow on ribbon at tip of flap. Glue ribbon rose on other end of ribbon "string."

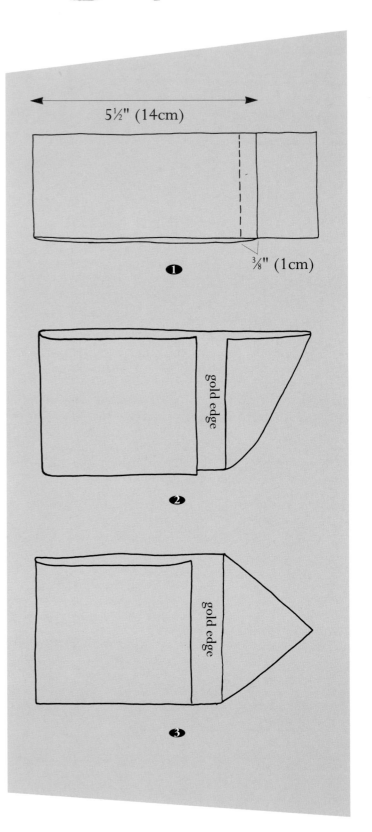

CHAPTER FOUR

Special Occasions with Ribbons

"There's a ribbon round my heart strings; it's
knotted at the end. It starts around my heart and
soul, and ends with you, my friend."

—Anonymous

Tabletop Mini-Topiaries

Stars and spheres become glittering table decorations when potted
and trimmed with narrow metallic ribbons.

RIBBON

- 2¼ yards (2m) each of ³⁄₁₆-inch-wide (4.5mm) metallic ribbons in 2 coordinating patterns
- 2¼ yards (2m) each of ⅛-inch-wide (3mm) metallic sheer ribbon in 2 colors
- 1½ yards (1.5m) of ⅝-inch-wide (1.5cm) gold wire-edge ribbon for bows

OTHER MATERIALS

- Papier-mâché star ornaments, approximately 4 inches (10cm) across
- 3 Styrofoam balls, 2½ inches (6.5cm) each (1 for topiary, 2 for filling inside of pots)
- 3 terra cotta flower pots, 2¾-inch (7cm) diameter each
- ⅜-inch-diameter (1cm) wood dowel, 18 inches (45.5cm) long, painted gold
- Gold and silver leaf
- Sheet moss
- 2 brass gold star and moon charms
- 3 small gold doilies
- Clear spray sealer and adhesive
- Hot glue gun and glue sticks

INSTRUCTIONS

1. Following manufacturer's instructions, spray adhesive on terra cotta pots and let dry until tacky. Lay gold leaf on base of pot and silver leaf on rim as desired. Smooth on to adhere. Continue until outside surfaces and inside rim are covered with leaf.

2. Spray gilded pots with a clear sealer.

3. Cut dowel into three 6-inch (15cm) lengths.

4. Poke a 1-inch (2.5cm) hole into base of stars and ball. Hot glue dowel to star and ball shapes, making sure dowel is straight.

5. Apply glue to surface of stars and ball. Cover with sheet moss, pressing moss in place to secure.

6. Cut an equal number of ³⁄₁₆-inch-wide (4.5mm) ribbons in 9½-inch (24cm) lengths for ball topiary. Starting at base where ball meets the dowel, glue the ribbon around ball until all ribbons are used. For the stars, cut an equal number of ⅛-inch-wide (3mm) ribbons in a variety of lengths, and wrap around the shape as desired. Glue in place.

7. Glue the sun and moon charms to center front of star shapes.

8. Cut two 3-inch (7.5cm) Styrofoam balls in half. Place dome side down into gilded pots. Cut a 3-inch (7.5cm) center from gold doily to place over Styrofoam surface. Hot glue in place around edge of pot to secure. Place topiary dowel unit in center of Styrofoam-filled pot, pushing dowel down about 1 inch (2.5cm). Secure with hot glue.

9. Tie a two-loop bow as instructed on page 17 at base of topiary with 18 inches (45.5cm) of gold wire-edge ribbon.

Ribbon Pieced Stocking

Ribbons pieced together take on the look of an exquisite fabric that has been cut and sewn and will form a stocking that will be cherished for years to come.

RIBBON

- 1 yard (1m) each of 1½-inch-wide (4cm) ribbons in 4 to 6 assorted Christmas and sheer patterns
- 2 yards (2m) of 1½-inch-wide (4cm) wire-edge ribbon for ruffle and bow
- 1 yard (1m) of 1½-inch-wide (4cm) ribbon for bow lining
- 1 yard (1m) of ¾-inch-wide (2cm) gold metallic ribbon for binding
- 9 inches (23cm) of ⅝-inch-wide (1.5cm) wire-edge taffeta ribbon
- 12 purchased small gold roses

OTHER MATERIALS

- ½ yard (45.5cm) of red satin fabric
- ½ yard (45.5cm) of red velvet backing fabric
- ½ yard (45.5cm) of lining fabric
- ½ yard (45.5cm) of batting
- 3½ yards (3.5m) of cording
- 3 large bells
- Decorative metallic and sewing threads

Stocking Pattern (for Ribbon Pieced Stocking and
Woven Stocking with Button Cuff)

One Square = One Inch
Enlarge 154%

INSTRUCTIONS

1. Using pattern on page 94, and following strip piecing directions on page 29, cut 1 stocking from red satin fabric, batting, and velvet. Make sure stocking toe in red satin fabric and batting both point to the left, and stocking toe in velvet points right. Cut 2 stockings from lining.

2. Draw a 45-degree angle line across the satin. Baste the batting to the wrong side of the satin.

3. Following strip piecing instructions, stitch ribbons to satin. Embellish as desired with decorative stitches and thread. Cover the entire front of stocking with ribbons.

4. With right sides together, stitch stocking front to back. Trim seams and clip curves. Turn right side out. Press. Hand tack or glue cord to seamed edge.

5. With right sides together, stitch lining pieces. Insert lining into stocking. Baste upper edges of lining and stocking together.

6. To create ruffle, cut a 1-yard (1m) strip of 1½-inch-wide (4cm) wire-edge ribbon and seam ends together. Knot one end of wire while pulling other end of wire, gathering ribbon to fit upper edge of stocking. Stitch ruffle to stocking. Fold a 9-inch (23cm) length of ribbon in half to form loop. Attach behind ruffle at upper edge corner.

7. Cut ¾-inch-wide (2cm) gold metallic ribbon in half. Stitch 1 strip of gold ribbon to each side of stocking upper edges, covering raw edges and ruffle seam.

8. With wrong sides together, fuse 1½-inch-wide (4cm) bow and lining ribbons together. Handstitch cord to both edges. Make a two-loop bow as instructed on page 17, and knot. Tack bells in center and join bow to base of stocking loop.

9. Stitch or glue roses along center of ribbons as desired.

Woven Stocking with Button Cuff

Ribbon weaving creates a simple but elegant basketweave effect for this button-cuffed Christmas stocking.

RIBBON

- 5½ yards (5m) each of ⅞-inch-wide (2cm) metallic ribbons in 2 coordinating patterns

OTHER MATERIALS

- 12-by-16-inch (30.5 by 40.5cm) piece of fusible interfacing
- ½ yard (45.5cm) of gold fabric for backing and lining
- Matching thread
- 2 packages of "crafty buttons"

INSTRUCTIONS

1. Lay interfacing adhesive side up. Cut twelve 16-inch (40.5cm) strips of ribbon in one color for vertical ribbons. From second color, cut sixteen 16-inch (40.5cm) strips for horizontal ribbons. Weave rectangle in basic weave as instructed on page 27. Fuse ribbons to interfacing.

2. Trace stocking pattern from page 94 on right side of woven ribbon rectangle, making sure stocking toe points to the right. Stitch along mark, then cut just outside of stitching.

3. For stocking back and lining, cut 3 stockings from gold fabric, 2 with toe to the left and 1 with toe to the right.

4. With right sides together, pin woven stocking front to stocking back. Stitch along sides and bottom in a ¼-inch (6mm) seam. Stitch lining together in same manner. Clip curves. Turn stocking right side out. Turn raw edges under ¼ inch (6mm) on upper edges of stocking and lining.

5. Make a 6-inch (15cm) loop from remaining ribbon and pin at top edge of stocking. Place lining into stocking and pin in place around top edge. Stitch in place.

6. Attach 4 rows of various gold and metal buttons to each woven section to form button cuff.

Gift Box Ornament

The ribbons on this loopy bow ornament were inspired by the glitter of gold.

RIBBON

- 2¼ (2m) yards of ⅞-inch-wide (2cm) metallic novelty ribbon
- 1½ yards (1.5m) of ⅞-inch-wide (2cm) metallic wire-edge ribbon cut in half
- ½ yard (45.5cm) of gold cording

OTHER MATERIALS

- 6-by-13-inch (15 by 33cm) piece of velveteen fabric
- 3-inch (7.5cm) square of floral foam
- Low-temperature glue gun and glue sticks

INSTRUCTIONS

1. Wrap foam square with fabric and glue. Wrap and glue ⅞-inch (2cm) metallic novelty ribbon around sides of box. Tie ends of cording together for hanger and glue to top of box.

2. Cut remaining length of ⅞-inch (2cm) metallic novelty ribbon in half and make 2 four-loop bows as instructed on page 17. Make 2 additional four-loop bows from ⅞-inch (2cm) metallic wire-edge ribbon. Wire centers of all 4 bows together. Glue to top of box.

Jeweled Ball Ornament

Gold-edged sheer ribbons combined with gemstones and gold balls will create a dazzling display for your tree.

RIBBON

- 1 yard (1m) of ⅝-inch-wide (1.5cm) royal blue satin ribbon cut into thirds

- 1 yard (1m) of ⅜-inch-wide (1cm) gold and purple metallic novelty ribbon cut into thirds

- 1½ yards (1.5m) of ⅞-inch-wide (2cm) navy gold-edge sheer ribbon cut in half

- ¼ yard (23cm) of ⅛-inch-wide (3mm) metallic grosgrain ribbon

OTHER MATERIALS

- 4-inch (10cm) gold ball ornament

- 8 round blue acrylic jewels

- Low-temperature glue gun and glue sticks

INSTRUCTIONS

1. Glue 2 lengths of blue satin ribbon vertically around ball, spacing evenly. Center and glue ⅜-inch-wide (1cm) ribbon over satin ribbon.

2. Glue a length of satin horizontally around center of ball. Center and glue ⅜-inch-wide (1cm) ribbon over satin ribbon.

3. Glue jewels around center of ball, spacing evenly. Tie ends of ⅛-inch-wide (3mm) ribbon together to make hanging loop and glue to top of ball.

4. With ⅞-inch-wide (2cm) navy sheer ribbon, make 2 four-loop bows as instructed on page 17. Glue bows to top of ball.

Poinsettia Gift Box

*Gold-edged ribbon poinsettias festively decorate a package and can
also be used to add to the Christmas decor.*

RIBBON

- ½ yard (45.5cm) of ⅞-inch-wide (2cm) red and gold taffeta ribbon cut into three 6-inch (15cm) lengths
- 1 yard (1m) of 1½-inch-wide (4cm) red and gold taffeta ribbon cut into four 8-inch (20.5cm) lengths
- ⅞-inch-wide (2cm) sheer gold-edge ribbon, enough to wrap box plus 2½ yards (2.5m) for bow

OTHER MATERIALS

- 4mm gold beads
- Box wrapped in gold paper

INSTRUCTIONS

1. Tie sheer ribbon around box, leaving streamers about 6 inches (15cm) long. With sheer ribbon, make an eight-loop bow as instructed on page 17, and wire onto knot.

2. Make a ribbon poinsettia as instructed on page 25. Glue to center of bow.

Ribbon Rose Gift Box

Beautiful and easy to make, a ribbon rose makes a lovely addition to any gift box.

RIBBON

- 1 yard (1m) of 1½-inch-wide (4cm) red and gold wire-edge ribbon
- ⅔ yard (61cm) of 1½-inch-wide (4cm) green and gold wire-edge ribbon
- Elan gold metallic mesh ribbon, enough to wrap box plus 18 inches (45.5cm) for bow

OTHER MATERIALS

- Box wrapped in gold paper
- Craft glue

INSTRUCTIONS

1. Glue lengths of mesh ribbon around box. With remaining 18-inch (45.5cm) length of ribbon, fold ends toward center and wire to form a two-loop bow as instructed on page 17. Glue to top of box. Fan out loops of ribbon.

2. Cut green and gold wire-edge ribbon into four 6-inch (15cm) lengths and make a gathered leaf from each, as instructed on page 21. Glue to center of bow. With red and gold wire-edge ribbon, and following the directions on page 22, make a large gathered rose and glue to center of bow.

Holly and Berries Gift Box

Holly and berries made with ribbons add a festive holiday touch to a special gift package.

RIBBON

- 1½-inch-wide (4cm) striped wire-edge ribbon, enough to wrap box plus ¾ yard (69cm) for bow
- ⅓ yard (30.5cm) of 1½-inch-wide (4cm) green and gold wire-edge ribbon
- ⅓ yard (30.5cm) of 1½-inch-wide (4cm) red and gold wire-edge ribbon

OTHER MATERIALS

- Box wrapped with gold paper
- 3 cotton balls or Fiberfil
- Craft glue

INSTRUCTIONS

1. Tie striped ribbon around box. Make a four-loop bow from striped ribbon as instructed on page 17.

2. Make holly leaves and berries as instructed on page 23. Glue holly leaves and berries to the center of bow.

Poinsettia Gift Box, Ribbon Rose Gift Box, Holly and Berries Gift Box

Harvest Basket

This basket will be the perfect accent to your harvest time decor.

RIBBON

- 5 yards (4.5m) of 2½-inch-wide (6.5cm) sheer wire-edge ribbon
- 5 yards (4.5m) of 2½-inch-wide (6.5cm) printed wire-edge ribbon
- 1½ yards (1.5m) of 1½-inch-wide (4cm) printed ribbon

OTHER MATERIALS

- Grapevine wall basket and floral foam
- Assorted ivy leaf picks, silk fall flowers, and stems
- Assorted artificial fall fruits, nuts and berries, lacquered fall picks
- Spanish moss

- Low-temperature glue gun and glue sticks

INSTRUCTIONS

1. Glue floral foam into basket and cover with moss. Insert ivy leaf picks into foam. Fill with flowers, pinecones, apple picks, and lacquered fall picks. Pull apart berry stems and glue into arrangement.

2. Cut a 3-yard (3m) length from both 2½-inch-wide (6.5cm) sheer wire-edge ribbon and 2½-inch-wide (6.5cm) printed wire-edge ribbon. Following the instructions on page 17, make a six-loop bow with one extra-long streamer from both ribbons and wire together. From 1½-inch-wide (4cm) printed ribbon, make a florist bow as instructed on page 17, and wire to 2 previous bows. Wire completed bow to wreath. Glue streamers in place, using photograph as reference.

3. Glue a flower, fruit pick, and berry stem in the center of bow.

4. From remaining ribbon lengths, and following the directions on page 17, make 2 four-loop bows with streamers. Attach bows and streamers together. Glue to right side of basket allowing streamers to hang.

5. Add remaining ivy, flowers, and fruit or berry picks.

Christmas Wreath

You'll be the envy of your neighborhood when this ribboned wreath decorates your door.

RIBBON

- 3½ yards (3.5m) of 4-inch-wide (10cm) Christmas plaid wire-edge ribbon
- 6 yards (5.5m) of 2½-inch-wide (6.5cm) Christmas plaid wire-edge ribbon
- 6 yards (5.5m) of 2½-inch-wide (6.5cm) red sheer wire-edge ribbon
- 3 yards (3m) of 2½-inch-wide (6.5cm) green sheer wire-edge ribbon
- 7½ yards (7m) of 2½-inch-wide (6.5cm) gold stretch ribbon

OTHER MATERIALS

- Large evergreen wreath
- Assorted fruit picks, silk poinsettias, and gold pinecones
- Large gold cherub
- Hot glue gun and glue sticks

INSTRUCTIONS

1. With 4-inch-wide (10cm) plaid wire-edge ribbon, make a large florist bow as instructed on page 17. Make 2 six-loop bows, one using long streamers from 2½-inch-wide (6.5cm) plaid ribbon and the other using 2½-inch-wide (6.5cm) red sheer ribbon, following the directions on page 17. Wire all 3 ribbons together. Wire bows to top of wreath, just off center.

2. From gold stretch ribbon, make 2 four-loop bows with long streamers. Wire one bow above and below upper bow. Form streamers from 2 lengths of green sheer ribbon and glue on either side of large bow. Arrange streamers around wreath and glue in place.

3. Using photograph as guide, glue poinsettias, pinecones, and fruit picks to wreath.

4. Bring one long gold stretchy streamer from top of wreath and twist it to bottom. Glue in place. Glue gold cherub on the top of this streamer.

Spring Swag

Your home can feel like spring year-round with the help of this lovely floral swag.

RIBBON

- 6¾ yards (6.5m) of 1½-inch-wide (4cm) pink sheer ribbon
- 2¾ yards (2.5m) of 1½-inch-wide (4cm) floral wire-edge ribbon

OTHER MATERIALS

- Swag
- 4 silk lavender hydrangeas
- 6 assorted silk roses and buds
- Assorted dry flowers and leaves
- Novelty wire pocketbook filled with moss (optional)
- Bird (optional)
- Wire

INSTRUCTIONS

1. Cut sheer pink ribbon into two 1-yard (1m) lengths, two 1¼-yard (1m) lengths, and one 2¼-yard (2m) length. Cut floral ribbon into one 1¼-yard (1m) length and one 1½-yard (1.5m) length. From each 1-yard (1m) length and following the instructions on page 17, make a four-loop bow with 10-inch (25.5cm) tails; from each 1¼-yard (1m) length, make a six-loop bow with 10-inch tails (25.5cm); from the 2¼-yard (2m) length, make a six-loop bow with 20-inch (51cm) tails. Cut all ends to form a V.

2. Wire the six-loop bow with 20-inch (51cm) tails to center top of swag. Wire floral ribbon bow just below the first bow. The 2 four-loop bows should be wired at either end of swag. Wire final 2 bows as photographed.

3. Using photograph as a guide, glue silk and dried flowers between bows on swag.

4. Cut remaining length of 1½-inch-wide (4cm) floral ribbon into several equal lengths. Loop and tie or glue lengths and sheer ribbon tails onto swag, filling in any empty spaces.

5. Wire bird to moss-filled pocketbook and wire both to center of swag.

Rainbow Notecard and Envelope

Send a special Valentine message to the one you love with this colorful notecard and envelope.

RIBBON

- 1 yard (1m) of ⅜-inch-wide (1cm) satin rainbow ribbon

OTHER MATERIALS

- 4¼-by-5½-inch (11 by 14cm) note card and matching envelope
- Embroidery needle and floss

INSTRUCTIONS

1. Draw a heart shape, approximately 2 by 2 inches (5 by 5cm), in center of note card. Draw 6 vertical lines inside heart outline, spacing lines ¼ inch (6mm) apart. Carefully cut along each vertical line as shown in diagram. Cut lines at sides of heart under which ribbon ends will go.

2. Cut three 2½-inch (6.5cm) lengths of ribbon. Weave ribbon lengths in and out of slits in center of heart in basic weave pattern as instructed on page 27. Glue raw edges to inside of note card. Using embroidery floss, stitch a long straight stitch around heart, securing raw ends of ribbon in stitching.

3. Cut a 9-inch length (23cm) of ribbon and tie a simple bow. Glue to bottom center of heart.

4. For envelope, measure in ¾ inch (2cm) from edge of envelope flap and draw a line parallel to edge. Draw another line ⅜ inch (1cm) away from first line.

5. Measure in ½ inch (1.5cm) from one side edge of flap, and draw a vertical line connecting top and bottom lines.

Draw another vertical line ½ inch (1.5cm) away from first vertical line, then ¼ inch (6mm) away from second line. Draw vertical lines every ½ inch (1.5cm), then ¼ inch (6mm) across horizontal lines 5 more times, ending with a line ½ inch (1.5cm) away from other side of flap. Cut along lines as for note card. Weave remaining ribbon in basic weave pattern through slits. Glue raw ends to underside of envelope flap. See page 88 for finished project.

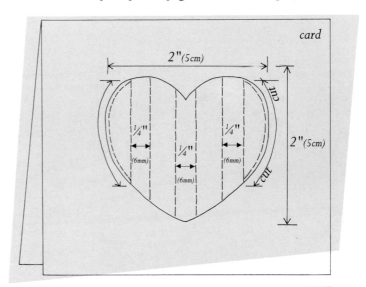

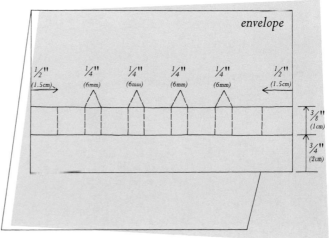

Party Basket

Life's a party when you give this special basket of goodies as a gift.

RIBBON

- ½ yard (45.5cm) each of ¾-inch-wide (2cm) ribbon for bows on dowels
- Additional ribbon to wrap dowels, approximately ½ to 1 yard (45.5cm to 1m) for each dowel
- ¾ yard (69cm) of ¾-inch-wide (2cm) ribbon to wrap balls
- 1½ yard (1.5m) of 1½-inch-wide (4cm) sheer blue ribbon for bow on handle
- 2 yards (2m) each of 1½-inch-wide (4cm) ribbons for florist bows
- Assorted ribbons in various widths and lengths to decorate gift boxes and bears and as decorations.

OTHER MATERIALS

- 12-inch (30.5cm) oval basket with floral foam in base
- Assorted party novelty items, such as party horns, flowers, animals, bears, and metallic grass
- Styrofoam balls, approximately 3 inches (7.5cm) in diameter
- Dowel cut into various lengths
- Assorted wrapped gift boxes
- Glitter
- Floral wire
- Low-temperature glue gun and glue sticks

INSTRUCTIONS

1. Tie gift boxes with ribbon. Place boxes in basket and arrange at different angles and heights.

2. Dress bears with ribbon by adding bows, scarves, and sashes. Wrap ribbon around bear as a romper, or trim a paper hat with ribbon. Use photograph for inspiration. Secure bears in basket by wiring to the gift boxes and placing close to handle for extra support.

3. Use grass to hide block in bottom of basket. Insert some grass into party horns and around basket as filler.

4. Brush Styrofoam balls with glue and then roll in glitter. Poke a 1-inch (2.5cm) hole into bottom of ball and insert dowel. Glue in place. Wrap dowel or ball with ribbon if desired. Attach a bow at base of ball where dowel is inserted. Insert dowels into basket base and glue to secure.

5. From blue sheer ribbon, make a simple two-loop bow with 18-inch tail as instructed on page 17. Attach to basket handle. Drape streamers around handle. Make florist bows from remaining 1½-inch-wide (4cm) ribbons using the directions on page 17 and attach to basket.

Party Bags and Wrappings

These decorative packages will create loads of excitement for their lucky recipients.

RIBBON

- Assorted ribbons to decorate boxes and bags (Actual amount needed will depend on size of bag or box to be decorated. The instructions indicate approximate amounts.)
- Assorted purchased bows and ribbon roses

OTHER MATERIALS

- Solid color gift bags and wrapping paper (excluding any with glossy finishes)
- Rubber stamps and ink
- Coordinating tissue paper and blank cards

INSTRUCTIONS

1. Stamp lengths of assorted ribbon as instructed on page 26. Stamp coordinated wrapping paper, paper bags, tissue paper, and cards that may be used with the ribbon. For variety, reverse colors, change the angle of stamp, add a new stamp, or combine stamps and colors.

2. Decorate bags as desired. Suggestions include punching holes in bags to weave 18-inch (45.5cm) lengths of stamped ribbon through; gluing ends inside bag or gluing to front and covering with a bow; making a rose as instructed on page 21 or 22 with 18- to 22-inch (45.5 to 56cm) lengths of stamped ribbon and gluing to bag or box. Add two-loop bows (see page 17) or florist bows (also on page 17) to packages with ribbon lengths ranging from 12 to 36 inches (30.5 to 1m).

CHAPTER FIVE

Ribbon Fashions

"Around her waist, she wore a yellow ribbon..."

—Civil War Ballad

Rose Splendor Slippers

Combine several familiar embroidery stitches to create this fanciful rose motif on soft, comfortable slippers.

RIBBON

- 1 package of 7mm Silk-Ease embroidery ribbon in colonial rose
- 1 package each of 4mm Silk-Ease embroidery ribbon in ultra violet, light orchid, mint, and dark moss

OTHER MATERIALS

- 1 pair black velvet or cloth slippers
- Size 20 chenille needle
- Size 10 embroidery needle
- White dressmaker's marking pencil
- Coin (about ⅞ inch in diameter)
- 1 package each of seed beads in rose and light rose
- Rose sewing thread

Shown actual size

INSTRUCTIONS

NOTE: Use chenille needle for ribbon work and embroidery needle to attach beads.

1. Using the design below as a guideline, mark the area for the large pink flower. Place the coin on the slipper. Lightly trace around the outside of the coin with the marking pencil. Using small thin lines or dots, mark the leaves and other flowers after you have stitched the center flower.

2. Work the lazy daisy stitch (see page 16) to make flower petals with the colonial pink ribbon. Place the center top stitch of the lazy daisy a little off center to create the folded look of the petals.

3. Using mint ribbon and the Japanese flower stitch (see page 16), work the leaves of the center flower.

4. Using light orchid, ultra violet, and dark moss ribbons, work French knots (see page 15) on each side of the center flower. Refer to photograph on previous page for placement of each ribbon color.

5. Use the rose sewing thread to attach the glass seed beads to form clusters. Place a dark rose bead in the center of each cluster and 5 light rose beads around the center bead. Sew through each bead twice, making sure they are secure.

Pouf Purse

Through the magic of ribbon weaving and ribbon piecing,
an evening bag can become a cherished possession.

RIBBON

- ¾ yard (69cm) each of 6 assorted ribbons for pouf section, 1¼- to 2½-inches (3.5 to 6.5cm) wide

- 1½ yards (1.5m) each of 7 assorted ribbons for woven flap, ⅛- to ½-inch (3mm to 1.5cm) wide

OTHER MATERIALS

- ½ yard (45.5cm) of moiré fabric

- ½ yard (45.5cm) of interfacing

- 1 yard (1m) of ⅜-inch (1cm) novelty cording

- ½ yard (45.5cm) of ¼-inch-wide (6mm) novelty cording

- Gold metallic and sewing thread

- Magnetic bag snap

- Decorative button

INSTRUCTIONS

1. To make a paper pattern for bag base, back, and lining, draw a 12-inch (30.5cm) half-circle and add 2 inches (5cm) to the straight edge. To make paper pattern for flap and lining, draw a 5¾-inch (14.5cm) half-circle with 2 inches (5cm) added to the straight edge. For a paper pattern of the bag insert, draw a 5¾-inch (14.5cm) half-circle with 1½ inches (4cm) added to straight edge. From moiré fabric, cut 3 of bag base pattern, 1 of flap pattern, and 1 of bag insert pattern.

2. Cut pouf section ribbons into 6½-inch (16.5cm) lengths. Arrange ribbons in desired order. Following strip piecing instructions on page 29, butt edges and zigzag stitch to join all into one piece for pouf section, measuring 6½ by 30 to 36 inches (16.5 by 76cm to 91cm).

3. Gather upper edge of pouf section to fit around lower edge of bag insert. With right sides together, stitch pouf section to bag insert. Apply snap section to bag insert. Gather lower edge of pouf section to fit around curved edges of bag back. Stitch in place.

4. Weave the narrow ribbons to make a 6½-inch-square (16.5cm) flap piece as instructed on page 27. Trace flap pattern onto woven square. Stitch on traced lines and cut just outside of stitching. Apply snap section to flap lining. With right sides together, stitch flap to lining along curved edges. Turn flap right side out and hand-stitch cord to curved edge.

5. With right sides together, stitch flap to bag back, centering flap to cover bag insert on front. Baste handle ends to back on either side of flap.

6. With right sides together, stitch lining front and back along curved edges. With right sides together, stitch bag and lining at upper edge, leaving an opening to turn.

7. Turn bag right side out and slipstitch opening closed. Add decorative button to bag front.

Woven Evening Bag

Rich jacquard and velvet ribbons are woven together in a delicate but versatile evening accessory.

RIBBON

- 4 yards (4m) each of 4 to 6 assorted ribbons, ⅜- to ⅞-inch (1 to 2cm) wide
- 8 yards (7.5m) of ⅛-inch-wide (3mm) metallic braid for drawstring and accent

OTHER MATERIALS

- 13-by-19-inch (33 by 48cm) rectangle and 8-inch (20.5cm) square of fusible interfacing (to weave and fuse ribbons)
- ½ yard (45.5cm) of moiré lining fabric
- Matching thread

INSTRUCTIONS

NOTE: Some ribbons in photograph are wire-edged. The wire may remain in ribbon or be removed before weaving for a softer look.

1. Cut ⅛-inch-wide (3mm) metallic braid in half and set aside one half. Use the other length for weaving. Cut approximately 25 warp ribbons in 12-inch (30.5cm) lengths and approximately 16 weft ribbons in 19-inch (48cm) lengths. Arrange ribbons in order desired and weave rectangle as instructed on page 27.

2. For the base of the bag, cut 7-inch (18cm) lengths of ribbon. Following same methods for bag, weave a 7-inch (18cm) square for base. Trace a 6½-inch (16.5cm) circle on this finished woven square. Stitch on traced lines. Cut just outside of stitching. Using this circle, cut 1 from fabric.

3. Stitch side seam of woven rectangle, leaving an opening for casing at third ribbon. Fold bag in half. Mark at fold and along third ribbon for opening for casing. Carefully slit horizontal ribbon and interfacing at this point. Fold edges of ribbon back, and stitch to vertical ribbons.

4. With right sides together, pin bag to bottom woven circle, clipping and easing to fit. Stitch.

5. Stitch lining side seam, leaving a 3-inch (7.5cm) opening near bottom for turning. With right sides together, stitch bag lining to bottom lining.

6. With right sides together, stitch upper edges of lining and bag. Turn right side out. Slipstitch opening closed. Press upper edge seam. Handstitch a length of metallic ribbon along seam.

7. To form casing, stitch on either side of third ribbon through lining and bag.

8. Cut remaining metallic braid into 2 lengths and slip 1 length through each side of the casing with safety pin. Knot ends of braid and loosen strands to form tassels.

Summer Hat with White Roses

You'll turn heads wearing this lavishly adorned ribbon rose hat.

RIBBON

- 1⅞ yards (2m) of 2-inch-wide (5cm) black velvet ribbon
- 5⅜ yards (5m) of 1½-inch-wide (4cm) wire-edge white taffeta ribbon
- 9¼ yards (8.5m) of 2¼-inch-wide (5.5cm) wire-edge taffeta ribbon

OTHER MATERIALS

- Purchased straw hat
- 2 stalks of baby's breath flowers
- 8 branches (3 leaves each) velvet rose leaves
- Hot glue gun and glue sticks

INSTRUCTIONS

1. From 1½-inch-wide (4cm) ribbon, cut 40 lengths, each 5 inches (13cm). From 2¼-inch-wide (5.5cm) ribbon, cut 40 lengths, each 6 inches (15cm). From each length, make a rolled petal as instructed on page 19. Finish and assemble 5 rolled petal roses as instructed on page 20.

2. From 2¼-inch-wide (5.5cm) ribbon, cut 15 lengths, 6 inches (15cm) each, for rosebuds. From each length, make a rolled petal. Make 5 three-petal rosebuds as instructed on page 20.

3. Wrap crown of hat with black velvet ribbon, centering ends at back. Glue band to hat. Trim excess ribbon.

4. From remaining velvet ribbon, make a two- or four-loop bow as instructed on page 17. Glue bow to back of hat.

5. Glue roses to front of hat. Add rosebuds as desired. Fill in with velvet leaves and baby's breath, gluing into place. Refer to photograph on previous page for placement.

Dogwood Pin

Simple flower-making techniques turn wire-edge taffeta ribbons into a lifelike dogwood branch lapel pin.

RIBBON

- ⅔ yard (61cm) of 1½-inch-wide (4cm) pink ombre wire-edge ribbon cut in half
- ⅓ yard (30.5cm) of 1½-inch-wide (4cm) green ombre wire-edge ribbon cut into four 3-inch (7.5cm) lengths

OTHER MATERIALS

- Bolo tie tip
- Pin back
- 2 large brown stamens
- Brown marker
- Matching thread
- Floral wire
- Brown floral tape
- Hot glue gun and glue sticks

INSTRUCTIONS

1. Mark each pink ombre ribbon length into four 3-inch (7.5cm) lengths. Make 2 stitched and gathered petals as instructed on page 21. Insert stamens in center. Attach to 3- to 4-inch (7.5 to 10cm) stem wire. To finish petals, cup outer edge of petal to inside. Using brown marker, make a small half-circle in "cup."

2. From green ribbon, make folded leaves as instructed on page 18. Twist ends slightly. Attach one leaf to one flower stem. Attach 3 leaves to second stem wire, covering completely with brown floral tape.

3. Secure 2 branches together with floral tape. Glue into tube of bolo tie tip. Glue pin back to back of bolo tie tip.

Rosewood Pin

This classic rose epitomizes romance and will add a lovely feminine touch to your jacket or blouse.

RIBBON

- ½ yard (45.5cm) of 1½-inch-wide (4cm) red wire-edge ribbon, cut into three 6-inch (15cm) lengths
- ⅓ yard (30.5cm) of ⅞-inch-wide (2cm) green ombre wire-edge ribbon, cut in half

OTHER MATERIALS

- Bolo tie tip
- Pin back
- Floral wire and floral tape
- Hot glue gun and glue sticks

Dogwood Pin, Rosewood Pin, Iris Pin

INSTRUCTIONS

1. From red wire-edge ribbon, make 3 rolled petals, (see page 19) and from green wire-edge ribbon, make 2 folded leaves (see page 18). Attach one petal at a time to stem wire. Overlap petals. Attach 2 leaves to another

stem wire and wire branches together. Cover edges with floral tape.

2. Trim stem as needed. Glue inside tie tip. Glue pin back to back of bolo tie tip.

Iris Pin

Capture the lasting beauty of spring irises in lilac-shaded wire-edge ombre ribbons.

OTHER MATERIALS

- 3-inch (7.5cm) bolo tie tip
- Pin back
- 1 yellow chenille stem
- Hot glue gun and glue sticks
- Floral wire and floral tape

INSTRUCTIONS

1. For leaves, cut ⅝-inch-wide (1.5cm) green ombre wire-edge ribbon into two 7-inch (18cm) lengths and one 9-inch (23cm) length. Make 3 boat leaves as instructed on page 20.

2. For each iris, cut ⅝-inch-wide (1.5cm) ombre wire-edge ribbon into three 4-inch (10cm) lengths and three 3½-inch (9cm) lengths. Make 2 irises as instructed on page 24, and wire to 2 stems. Add 1 leaf to 1 flower stem. Cover wires with floral tape. Attach 2 leaves to remaining flower stem. Cover irises with floral tape

3. Insert into bolo tie tip. Trim stems and glue in place. Glue pin back to bolo tie tip.

RIBBON

- ⅝ yard (57.5cm) each of ⅝-inch-wide (1.5cm) ombre wire-edge ribbon in green and 2 shades of purple

White Beret with Ribbon Embroidery

Gold-edged sheers and embroidery ribbons combine in this dramatic motif on a classic wool beret.

RIBBON

- 1 package each of 4mm Silk-Ease embroidery ribbon in spring moss, light pink, and cream
- 1 package of 7mm Silk-Ease embroidery ribbon in moss
- 2 packages of 15mm ultra-sheer embroidery ribbon in light coral
- 1 package of 15mm ultra-sheer embroidery ribbon in tea rose

OTHER MATERIALS

- Purchased beret
- Water-soluble pen
- 1 package embroidery floss in light pink
- Embroidery needles, tapestry needles

INSTRUCTIONS

1. Transfer design to beret using water-soluble pen. Embroider the leaves in fly stitch, using 4mm and 7mm Silk-Ease embroidery ribbon. Refer to photograph on previous page.

2. For the main flower, work a base of straight stitches in circular pattern with embroidery floss. The second and third rings of the circle are evenly spaced blanket stitches (see page 16) made with embroidery floss. The final ring is stitched in the lazy daisy stitch (see page 16) with light pink 4mm Silk-Ease embroidery ribbon. Fill inner circle with a mixture of light pink and cream French knots (see page 15) made with 4mm Silk-Ease embroidery ribbon. The 15mm ultra-sheer novelty ribbon is loosely woven through the floss webbing.

3. With tapestry needle and ultra-sheer embroidery ribbon in light coral, whipstitch the edges of the beret. Referring to photograph, add French knots to outer edges of flower design.

Embroidery Pattern

Burgundy Hat with Flowers

Give a timeless rolled-brim hat a dash of style with a bouquet of richly colored ribbon roses nestled in the brim.

RIBBON

- 2¾ yards (2.5m) of 1½-inch-wide (4cm) sheer novelty ribbon
- 1 yard (1m) of 1½-inch-wide (4cm) brown wire-edge ribbon
- 3¼ yards (3m) of 1½-inch-wide (4cm) burgundy wire-edge ribbon
- 1¼ yards (1m) of 2¼-inch-wide (5.5cm) burgundy wire-edge ribbon

OTHER MATERIALS

- Purchased hat
- 2 stamens
- Floral wire
- Floral tape
- Hot glue gun and glue sticks

INSTRUCTIONS

1. Wrap sheer novelty ribbon around hat and overlap ends at back. Glue in place. With remaining ribbon, make a florist bow with tails as instructed on page 17. Glue bow to back of hat at center seam.

2. Cut brown wire-edge ribbon into three 12-inch (30.5cm) lengths. Make 3 stitched leaves as instructed on page 20.

3. From 1½-inch-wide (4cm) wire-edge ribbon, cut 21 lengths, 5 inches (13cm) each, and from 2¼-inch-wide (5.5cm) wire-edge ribbon, cut 8 lengths, 6 inches (15cm) each. Make 29 rolled petals as instructed on page 19. Assemble petals into rolled-petal roses as follows: a 16-petal rose, an 8-petal rose, and two 3-petal rosebuds. See page 20 for directions.

4. Secure with floral wire. Cover all raw edges with floral tape.

5. Using the photograph on the next page as a guide, glue leaves and flowers to hat.

Sources

Look for the materials and supplies used in this book in fabric and craft stores nationwide. We'd like to thank the following companies for their assistance in providing us with some of the materials used in the projects.

Artificial Flowers
2328 Bath Avenue
Brooklyn, New York 11214

City Blossoms
17 Battery Place
New York, New York 10004

Coats and Clark
30 Patewood Drive
Greenville, South Carolina 29615

Concord Fabrics
1359 Broadway
New York, New York 10018

Fairfield Processing Corporation
88 Rose Hill
Danbury, Connecticut 06810

Ghees
2620 Centenary Boulevard
Shreveport, Louisiana 71104

Handcraft
Route 3, Box 73
Pharr, Texas 78577

Handler Textile Corporation
24 Empire Boulevard
Moonachie, New Jersey 07074

The Hiawatha Corporation
East 681 Johns Prairie Road
Shelton, Washington 98584

Houston Art and Frame, Inc.
P.O. Box 56146
Houston, Texas 77256

Kunin Felt
380 Lafayette Road
Hampton, New Hampshire 03843

Mine Hill
P.O. Box 1060
Janesville, Wisconsin 53547

Plaid Enterprises
1649 International Court
Norcross, Georgia 30091

Rosebar Textile Company, Inc.
93 Entin Road
Clifton, New Jersey 07014

Rosie's Creations
New York, New York
(212) 362-6069

V.I.P. Fabrics
1412 Broadway
New York, New York 10018

$\mathcal{I}ndex$

$\mathcal{B}$

Baskets, 102, *102*, 106, 107
Black Pansy Pillow, *32*, *33*, *33*
Bottles, *37*, 37–38
Boxes, 66, *66*, 67, *67*, *68*, 69, *69*, 97, *97*, 99, *100*, 101
Bridal Chair Back Swag, 76, 78, 79, *79*
Bridal Headpiece and Veil, 80, *81*, *82*
Bridal Topiary, 76, 77–78
Bridesmaid Headpiece, 83
Burgundy Hat with Flowers, 124, *125*

$\mathcal{C}$

Centerpieces, 55, *55*, 56
Christmas projects, 90–103
Christmas Wreath, 103, *103*
Cinched Pillow with Insets, 42, *42*, 43, *43*

$\mathcal{D}$

Daffodils in a Terra Cotta Pot, *48*, 49–50
Dogwood Pin, 120, *121*

$\mathcal{E}$

Embroidered Victorian Linens, 51–52, *53*
Embroidery, 11, 15, 51–52, *53*, 54, *122*, 123

$\mathcal{F}$

Fashion projects, 111–125
Flanged Pillow with Ribbon Weaving, 43, 44, *44*, 45

Flowers, 18, *18*, 104, *104*
    daffodils, 22, *22*, *48*, 49–50
    dahlias, 22, *22*, 34, *34*
    geraniums, *48*, 49
    hyacinths, 23, *23*, *48*, 50
    irises, 24, *24*, 121, *121*
    magnolias, 55, *55*, 56
    morning glories, 24, *24*
    pansies, 25, *25*, 35, *35*, 36, *36*
    petals, 19, *19*, 20, *20*, 21, *21*
    poinsettias, 25, *25*, 99, *100*
    roses, 20, *20*, 21, *21*, 22, *22*, 55, 56, 62, *63*, *64*, 99, *100*, 101, *112*, 113, *118*, 119, 124, 125
    stems, 21, *21*
    sweet peas, 25, *25*, 60, *61*
    violets, 47, *47*
Frames, 70, *70*

$\mathcal{G}$

Garlands, 62, *63*, *64*
Geraniums in a Terra Cotta Pot, *48*, 49
Gift Box Ornament, 97, *97*
Guest Book, 72, 73

$\mathcal{H}$

Harvest Basket, 102, *102*
Hats, *118*, 119, *122*, 123, 124, *125*
Holly and Berries Gift Box, *100*, 101
Humpty Dumpty Pillow and Wall Hanging, 38, *39*, 40–41
Hyacinths in a Terra Cotta Pot, *48*, 50

$\mathcal{I}$

Iris Pin, 121, *121*

$\mathcal{J}$

Jeweled Ball Ornament, 98, *98*
Jewelry, 120, 121, *121*

$\mathcal{K}$

Key to My Heart Sachet Pillow, 72, 74

$\mathcal{L}$

Lamps, 60, *61*
Large Heart Pillow with Dahlias, 34, *34*
Leaves, 20, *20*
    folded, 18, *18*
    holly, 23, *23*, *100*, 101
    pulled, 19, *19*
Linens, 51–52, *53*, 54, 57, *58*, 59, *59*
Looms, 9, 14

$\mathcal{M}$

Magnolia Centerpiece, 55, *55*, 56
Medium Heart Pillow with Pansies, 36, *36*

$\mathcal{O}$

Offray, Claudius Marie, 9, 11
Ornaments, 97, *97*, 98, *98*

Index

P

Party Bags and Wrappings, 108, *109*
Party Basket, *106*, 107
Photo Storage Box, 67, *67*, *68*
Pillows, *32*, 33, 34, *34*, 35, *35*, 36, *36*, 38, *39*, 42, *42*, 43, *43*, 71, *71*, *72*, 74
Pins, 120, 121, *121*
Place mats, 57, *58*, 59, *59*
Poinsettia Gift Box, 99, *100*
Potpourri, 85, 86, *87*
Pouf Purse, 114–115, *115*
Purses, 114–115, *115*, 116, *117*

R

Rainbow Notecard and Envelope, 105
Ribbon Embroidered Duvet, *53*, 54
Ribbon Pieced Stocking, 92, *93*, *94*, 95
Ribbon Rose Gift Box, 99, *100*, 101
Ribbons
 craft, 14
 cut edge, 14
 history of, 9–11
 merrowed-edge wire, 14
 metallic, 14
 patterned, 14
 printed, 14
 sheer, 14
 washable, 11, 14
 wire-edge, 11, 14
 woven edge, 14

Ring Bearer's Pillow, 71, *71*, 72
Rose Garland on a Chain, 62, *63*, 64
Rose Napkin Rings, *55*, 56
Rose Splendor Slippers, *112*, 113
Rosewood Pin, 120, 121, *121*

S

Slippers, *112*, 113
Small Heart Pillow with Pansies, *32*, 35, *35*
Small Square Box, 69, *69*
Special occasions projects, 89–110
Spring Swags, 104, *104*
Stamping, 26
Stationery, 105, *105*
Stitches, 15
Stockings, 92, *93*, *94*, 95, 96, *96*
Summer Hat with White Roses, *118*, 119
Supplies, 15
Swags, 76, 78, 79, *79*, 104, *104*
Sweet Pea Lamp and Shade, 60, *61*

T

Table runners, 57, *58*, 59, *59*
Tabletop Mini-Topiaries, 90, *91*, 92
Tea Bag Potpourri, 85, 86, *87*
Tea cozy, 57, *58*, 59, *59*
Tea Time Table Set, 57, *58*, 59, *59*
Techniques
 bows, 17, *17*
 embroidery, 15

Techniques (*cont.*)
 flowers, 18, *18*, 19, *19*, 20, *20*, 21, *21*, *22*, 22, 23, *23*, 24, *24*, 25, *25*
 leaves, 18, *18*, 19, *19*, 20, *20*, 23, *23*
 stamping, 26
 strip piecing, 29, *29*
 weaving, 27, 28, *28*
Topiaries, 76, 77–78, 90, *91*, 92
Tufted Pillow with Corner Ties, *43*, 45, *45*

V

Victorian Apothecary Bottles, 37–38, *37*
Victorian projects, 37–38, *37*, 51–52, *53*, 83, *84*, 85
Violets in a Demitasse Cup, 47, *47*

W

Wall hangings, 38, *39*, 40–41
Weaving, 27, *27*, 28, *28*, 43, 44, *44*, 45, 71, *71*, *72*, *93*, *94*, 96, *96*, 114–115, *115*, 116, *117*
Wedding Frame, 70, *70*
Wedding Heart Box, 66, *66*, 68
Wedding Nosegay, 83, *84*, 85
Wedding projects, 66–88
White Beret with Ribbon Embroidery, *122*, 123
Woven Evening Bag, 116, *117*
Woven Stocking with Button Cuff, *93*, *94*, 96, *96*
Wreaths, 103, *103*